"Marion McGovern has given us a wise and priceless GPS for the Gig Economy. She supplants business buzz words with clarity, lofty theory with seasoned experience, ungrounded projections with shoot-from-the-hip practicality, and lofty strategies with realistic tools for successful results. This careful, smart, and easy-to-read book draws you in and enables you to put its lessons to good use. Buy it. Apply it!"

—Louis Patler, president, The B.I.T. Group,
author of *Make Your Own Waves* and *If It Ain't Broke...Break It!*

"*Thriving in the Gig Economy* adeptly tackles the many faces of the independent workforce and offers valuable advice for professionals and clients alike. This book is a forward-thinking must-read for anyone considering working in the Gig Economy or for companies implementing an independent workforce program."

—Gene Zaino, CEO, MBO Partners

"*Thriving in the Gig Economy* is a must read for anyone interested in or associated with the future of work. If you're a 1099 worker trying to navigating the myriad of opportunities and pitfalls, you'll save yourself a lot of time and money by reading this book—Marion nails it."

—Chad Nitschke, CEO & cofounder of Bunker

"In *Thriving in the Gig Economy*, Marion McGovern offers expert, real world advice to those looking to take control of their career and make their way in the Gig Economy. As founder of one of the pioneering firms in the space, she knows well the possibilities and the hidden challenges of work untethered to the old fashioned "job." She lays out those details in an engaging and well-organized style. Read this book and get an edge in building a career and working life to fit our increasingly on demand world."

—Barry Asin, president, Staffing Industry Analysts (SIA)

"Whether you're an experienced professional looking for new opportunities or a college graduate struggling to find the right job, *Thriving in the Gig Economy* is the survival guide you need. The nature of work has changed, and this new model of workforce independence is an exciting development that supports more flexibility, security, and entrepreneurship. You need to read this book!"

—Cynthia Cleveland, CEO, Broadthink, Board Director

"This is your go-to source for a font of information about the Gig Economy—how to build your brand, set your price, find work that matches your skills, manage employment risks, and master the ecosystem that supports this fast-growing sector."

—Wayne F. Cascio, PhD, Distinguished Professor, University of Colorado,
and Robert H. Reynolds Chair in Global Leadership,
Editor, *Journal of International Business Studies*,
The Business School, University of Colorado–Denver

"If the Gig Economy hasn't affected you yet, it's about to. *Thriving in the Gig Economy* is a must read if you want to stay ahead of the economic transformation we're experiencing."

—Mike Faith, CEO, Headsets.com, Inc.

"*Thriving in the Gig Economy* is a must read for anyone considering becoming an independent consultant, a newly established consultant, or a seasoned consultant that truly wants to thrive, not just survive, in this evolving Gig Economy. Marion McGovern's entrepreneurial zeal and expertise establishing and running a successful business focused on this marketplace long before the term 'Gig Economy' was coined, coupled with her latest research on how this evolving economy is growing and changing, provides the reader with the tools, tips, techniques, and resources to truly thrive in the Gig Economy!"

—Jeff Hayes, president and CEO of CPP, Inc.

"I've known Marion professionally for over 25 years and watched her gain the respect of her peers entrepreneuring and innovating in the Human Capital world through many changes in the economy from the dotcom boom to bust and back to boom. Her insights on what we are now calling the Gig Economy are invaluable whether you are in the midst of running a business, getting back in the managerial game, or just trying to keep up with all the changes happening in the employment world. *Thriving in the Gig Economy* will provide invaluable insights and resonate with entrepreneurs, managers, and senior executives."

—Karen Behnke, founder, Juice Beauty

"Informative and easy to read, with a wealth of useful tips, great ideas, and cautionary advice for anyone interested in making the jump to the Gig Economy. Having just recently made that decision myself, I have found Marion's guidance to be timely and invaluable."

—Dirk Sodestrom, former managing partner of M Squared Consulting

"This book is like getting a MBA with a specialization in the Gig Economy. Marion writes with a depth and practicality that only a successful entrepreneur can bring to us. Let this be your guidebook for this rising segment of our economy."

—Atul Vashistha, chairman, Neo Group & Supply Wisdom

Thriving in the Gig Economy effortlessly informs the reader of the vast and ever-changing industry of how a hiring manager might secure talent or, alternatively, a consultant lands a project and all the complexities behind the scenes. She also defines the 'sharing and on-demand economies' of which there are a plethora of these services using technology without human contact."

—Michelle Boggs, CEO, McKinley Marketing Partners

Thriving in the Gig Economy makes a strong case for the smart use of consultants and the contingent workforce. It's a must-read for any C-Suite executive who is looking at the pros and cons of hiring versus contracting out for talent. And for the aspiring or new independent contractor, this book offers a detailed procedural on how to expertly set up your shop for success."

—Michael Cappelluti, president, The Highlands Consulting Group LLC

"Marion McGovern is a pioneer in the Gig Economy, having founded M Squared Consulting in 1988. During the past 30 years, the way we work has changed dramatically due to technology advances, globalization, and social changes, and Marion has been a leader the entire way. Her latest book, *Thriving in the Gig Economy*, is the most insightful analysis of our new world of work that I've read and it also includes very helpful recommendations for how we can thrive in it."

—Paul Witkay, founder and CEO, Alliance of CEOs

"From branding to financial management, McGovern delivers practical, nononsense insights for those seeking to strive in the new world of work or as consultants, gig workers, and solo entrepreneurs. A timely look at what it takes to strive in the new world of work from someone who has been ahead of the curve, and brings experience and practical ideas and practices for those focused on success. From building your brand to optimizing your financial results and personal satisfaction, McGovern offers practical ideas and practices for those seeking to strive in today's economy."

—Willa Seldon, partner, The Bridgespan Group

"All businesses will be affected by the Gig Economy, which offers great business promise yet so much confusion at the same time. *Thriving in the Gig Economy* provides all the information needed to ensure that any business of any size will be able to take advantage of this trend instead of being disrupted by it. This book is invaluable for anyone who recognizes how the Gig Economy represents both opportunity and risk. *Thriving in the Gig Economy* provides the larger context that explains the massive explosion of the Gig Economy and how it is reshaping businesses of all sizes. It also provides a thorough and well-researched operational guide for anyone who wants to take advantage of the Gig Economy to grow their business."

—Susan Butenhoff, CEO, Access Integrated Brand Communications

"Marion McGovern has given us a great roadmap for the future. As an entrepreneur and a pioneer in the high-end independent talent arena, she brings a unique perspective and reminds us all of the potential of this emerging market. A must read for anyone who wants to understand the Gig Economy and particularly the professional end of this category, which is so often overlooked."

—Jody Greenstone Miller, cofounder and CEO, Business Talent Group

THRIVING IN THE
GIG ECONOMY

THRIVING IN THE GIG ECONOMY

How to Capitalize and Compete
in the New World of Work

Marion McGovern

CAREER
PRESS
Wayne, NJ

THRIVING IN THE GIG ECONOMY
Edited by Jodi Brandon
Typeset by Diana Ghazzawi
Cover design by Howard Grossman/12e Design
Figure illustrations on cover by bloomua/depositphotos
Printed in the U.S.A.

To order this title, please call toll-free 1-800-CAREER-1 (NJ and Canada: 201-848-0310) to order using VISA or MasterCard, or for further information on books from Career Press.

The Career Press, Inc.
12 Parish Drive
Wayne, NJ 07470
www.careerpress.com

To my amazing family,
Jerry, Morgan, Nora, and Kevin.
Being part of our tribe is the best gig ever.

Acknowledgments

It occurred to me as I was writing this book that the process was a lot like starting a company. At the onset, the idea is totally in your head, evolving and growing as you ponder it more and more. At some point, you invite other people to the party, sharing your idea with them to get their reactions and opinions. Some of those comments you may take to heart, others you won't, because it is—after all—your idea. So you redefine and clarify the content, while documenting the questions yet to be answered. Then you make your plan for how you will turn this idea into a reality. You start doing the work to answer those questions, digging into the subject matter to reveal the truths that will help drive the initiative forward. For the non-fiction writer, that final step can be very people-intensive, because interviews with content experts are critical to refining the message.

> "I just want to thank everyone who made this day necessary."
> —Yogi Berra

At this point, though, the paths diverge, and interestingly the author's journey bears a bit more risk. The entrepreneur launches his product or service and relatively quickly gets feedback from the marketplace. Customer reception to certain features or functions may cause her to tweak the product to better meet client needs. Through a continuous feedback loop, the marketplace validates the product offering through its patronage.

The author, on the other hand, launches her writing process, revising not with marketplace input, but with deliberate literary flourishes. The author has no access to the continuous feedback loop that enables the entrepreneur to refine his service offering. So, the writer must go out on the proverbial limb and go with the book, without validation, but with hope that the message is clear comprehensive and meaningful.

My hope is strong because of all the people who have been involved along the way. To paraphrase Hillary Clinton, it takes a village to write a book. I was so lucky to have not just a village but a veritable metropolis at my disposal.

Thriving in the Gig Economy could not have been written without the time, insights, and opinions of so many subject matter experts. Many of them were old friends or colleagues whom I knew from the M Squared days. In fact, those meetings started with M Squared. I must say it was a bit ironic to interview Dirk Sodestrom, the general manager of M Squared, about his perspective on the world of independent expertise now and in the future. That said, it was perhaps one of my more important meetings, as it set the tone for me as an informed observer and no longer a participant. Dirk continued to be very helpful, providing me access to other team members and consultants, as well as allowing me to use the M Squared network as a key component of my independent consulting survey.

Readers may notice that I talk a great deal not just about M Squared, but also about Business Talent Partners and MBO Partners, because I have known them for years and trust their leadership, Jody Miller and Gene Zaino, respectively. Both of these key figures in the world of independent work were generous with their time and so helpful to me in the process. Similarly, Michelle Boggs of McKinley Marketing Partners was happy to reconnect after many years. My CEO Alliance colleagues were also willing to participate, in particular Cat Lincoln of Clever. Consultants, too, like Sandor Sochot, Nathan Banwart, and Chris Neal, as well as several others, were open to explaining their consulting paths. Similarly, YPO colleagues Ranjan Sinha, Mike Cappelluti, and Lesley Berglund let me share their stories.

Many of my interviews were with people with whom I had no connection. Several came from website inquiries. Although many companies turned me down (apparently WeWork won't talk to anyone on principle), several granted me access immediately. These include Vikram Ashok of SpareHire, Harpreet Singh of Experfy, Stewart Lewtan of Zintro, Chad

Nitschke of Bunker Insurance, Bridget Loudon and Paul Anderson of Expert360, Patrick Ambron of Brandyourself, Ken Baylor of Stealth Worker, Antonio Calabrese of Boonle, Mason Blake of UpCounsel, Stephen DeWitt of WorkMarket, Joey Fraser of Shortlist, Robert Jordan of the Interim Executive Association, Steven Holmes of Shift Pixy, and Catherine Fisher of LinkedIn.

Experts and pundits graciously shared their insights with me. Special thanks to Steve King of Emergent Research, Eamonn Kelley of Deloitte, Dr. Wayne Casio of the University of Colorado, Jacob Morgan of the Future of Work Organization, and George Gendron of The Solo Project.

Without the content experts, I would not have been able to build the body of knowledge that resulted in *Thriving in the Gig Economy*. However, without my readers, I would not have been able to share it in the best way. When I wrote my first book, I was still running M Squared, so I had a built-in editorial board by virtue of my employees. That was not the case with this book. A few months before the manuscript was due to my publisher, I realized that I needed other eyes on my manuscript. I needed people who knew the subject and could validate my viewpoints, as well as novices who could read it to see if my explanations made sense to those unfamiliar with the world of work. My former partners, Paula Reynolds and Claire McAuliffe, were masterful in the former role, because they were steeped in the foundation of the content so very adroit at questioning the newer material. A wonderful group of people, most notably Susan Lupica, Alison Hess, and Bill Murray, helped me in the latter case. Because I was talking about many digital issues, I wanted a cross-section of ages to be sure my stories and solutions made sense to various generations. My accomplished nieces Megan Massaron and Sara Naughton were my representatives of the GenX world. The Millennial lens was provided by my daughters, Morgan and Nora McGovern, who, in demonstrating their writing prowess, made me realize all of that money we spent on their education was well worth it.

At the very start of the project, my former board member Louis Patler was a great help in answering the question of whether to self-publish or not. Once the decision was "not," he also made the introduction to John Willig, my agent. John's counsel was valuable in helping me crystallize my message, target audience, and key selling points.

Finally, my wonderful, husband, Jerry, who did not quite understand why I chose to write the book when I could have just chosen to play more golf, was very supportive. He put up with missed meals, weekends spent writing, and some less-than-pleasant moods as my deadlines loomed. Now that it is all said and done, don't worry, dear: life will change. As a proud member of the Gig Economy myself, I work this way for both flexibility and control over my life. Now that *Thriving in the Gig Economy* is completed, my life is my own again, and I look forward to playing a little more golf.

Contents

Foreword

For 20 years, I had the best job in journalism. I led the creative team that built the *Inc.* magazine brand, created the *Inc. 500* ranking of the fastest-growing companies in the U.S., and launched *Inc.com*. During the 1980s and '90s, my colleagues and I had the privilege and thrill of documenting the transition from an industrial economy to one driven by entrepreneurship and innovation.

At first no one paid much attention to what we had to say. After all, we were a bunch of kids managing an upstart publication. Things changed when authorities such as Peter Drucker began to weigh in on what was happening. Drucker, for example, referred to the emergence of an entrepreneurial economy as "the most important development in the second half of the 20th century."

Well, there is another transition playing out right now. It is still in its infancy, but gaining momentum and bearing down on us all. In the title of this book, Marion McGovern refers to it as the "Gig Economy." At my new venture, The Solo Project, my partners and I refer to it as the "solo movement." Whatever you choose to call it, this transformation in how the work of the economy gets done is, in some ways, more significant than the one we were documenting at *Inc.* This one is personal, affecting us on a profoundly individual level.

I think of it this way. While our economy continues to create work, less and less of it comes to us packaged as "jobs." Thanks to the rapid change caused by technology and globalization, work is increasingly "chunked" into projects. Instead of going out and looking for a job, many of us find that the challenge is to figure out how to plug into this project economy. In other words, it's increasingly up to us not to find a job, but to design one for ourselves, and become responsible for creating our personal professional and financial security.

My partners and I have talked to or interviewed hundreds of individuals—including some of the smartest folks we know in business, finance, academia, and policy—who still think of this as some distant phenomenon, as in "the future of work." Well, as one of our favorite writers said, "the future is already here, it's just not evenly distributed."

Here are a few dispatches from this "future," from research my partners and I did, in partnership with the Knight Foundation, about the implications of the solo phenomenon for urban leaders:

- According to a recent RAND-Princeton University study, from 2005 to 2015 the traditional workforce, people working in full-time jobs, didn't grow at all. Meanwhile the population of people working in "alternative work arrangements" increased by 67 percent. The report concludes, "A striking implication of these estimates is that all of the net employment growth in the U.S. economy appears to have occurred in alternative work arrangements."

- The most recent annual Gallup workforce survey revealed that only 32 percent of American workers are engaged at work. At the same time, two-thirds of people working on their own report that they find their work fulfilling.

- Eighty percent of individuals who make the transition from traditional to indie work and last for 12 months on their own report they can't imagine ever returning to a traditional job. This includes "involuntary" soloists who went out on their own because they lost a job.

For some of us, this is thrilling. TED founder Richard Saul Wurman sums up the opportunity this way: "For the first time in human history, individuals can design a life around the pursuit of interesting work." My partners and I would add that we can do this interesting work with partners we admire and trust, and for clients we respect.

However, we understand that for many this transformation is terrifying, requiring whole new skill sets and attitudes. After all, we've been raised and educated to be good organization men and women.

What we need is a re-education, one that will help us collectively build the skills and characteristics necessary to flourish. If management thinking has been driven by the question "How do we make our organizations better?" we urgently need a new inquiry driven by the question "How do we make our *work* better?"

This book marks a smart beginning of that inquiry.

While the shelves are filled with self-improvement titles, this book is different. First off, and perhaps most important in the world of entrepreneurship, the ideas in this book are road-tested. You'll quickly see you're in the hands of someone who's spent the better part of her adult life creating structures and supports that enable other people's entrepreneurial ambitions. Back in the late 1980s, when independent professionals were still thought to be people who couldn't get a decent job, McGovern launched a wildly successful platform that created a market for independent consultants. McGovern's M Squared earned a spot on the *Inc. 500* ranking of fast-growth ventures, which is where my colleagues and I first met this remarkable woman.

In 1993, McGovern launched Collabrus, one of the first companies to tackle the unglamorous but crucial work of compliance and payroll services that enable independent contractor engagements. In 2001, she published *A New Brand of Expertise: How Independent Consultants Are Transforming the World of Work*. Today, with this book, she's still at it, packaging up her know-how to share with new generations of individuals in the pursuit of good work.

Entrepreneurship is not a job, it's a life. And choosing to work on one's own is every bit as much entrepreneurship as starting a venture-backed company. On a journey such as this one, you don't want a novice as an advisor. You want a veteran, who's been there, done that, and doesn't forget for a moment that the psychological and emotional challenges are as big as the strategic and the tactical. That's what you get with McGovern. This book is the next best thing to having McGovern on speed dial.

—GEORGE GENDRON

George Gendron was the editor-in-chief of Inc. Magazine for 20 years. He was the founder and director of the entrepreneurship center at Clark University in Massachusetts, and is the cofounder and managing director of The Solo Project, a new venture designed to support independent professionals and creatives.

Introduction

In the summer of 2015, I had a bit of an out-of-body experience. Three different inquiries came to me because of my experience building and running M Squared Consulting, a company I started in 1988 and sold in 2005, and for which I served as a board member until 2014. M Squared was an innovator in its day, being one of the first companies in the nation to match independent expertise to client project needs. We were in the Gig Economy before that ever became a term of art. Having been out of the company for two years, I was intrigued when I received this series of calls in the space of two months.

> "There is nothing new in the world, except the history you do not know."
>
> —Harry S. Truman

One overture came from a venture capitalist interested in building a marketplace platform for professional women who had left the workforce for family reasons. The platform would find them gigs, train them in the newest workplace tools, and provide a working mother forum. Another was from a private equity firm that wanted to create a marketplace platform for on-demand energy industry workers in eastern Africa. Staffing the oil fields was tough, so creating a qualified buffer of potential workers could smooth production issues. The final notion was from a pair of successful entrepreneurs in the technology space who were developing a marketplace platform for entry level professional hires that would eliminate the need for human oversight in the recruiting process. Like the common application in the college application process, this artificially intelligent front end would identify the best applicant for junior management–level hires.

All three of these ventures shared the "marketplace platform" element. At least one, the recruiting site, was being viewed as a major disruption to the current environment. The other two were viewed as an opportunity to target an underserved segment of a large marketplace. Perhaps most importantly, all three were technology plays being launched by technologists. The fact that these platforms were being created for human capital was not relevant to the enterprise. Even more simply, the services being developed were being built by guys who had never operated—nor funded—a service business, not even software as a service.

Given that a hallmark of my company was the high-touch service we provided our clients in the structuring of virtual consulting engagements, my focus in each of these discussions was around the human element of the process. I brought up questions about the nature of the interactions with the female consultants, oil field workers, and recruits, challenging why they would affiliate with the sites. I wondered why companies would patronize the service and discovered that sales models for the demand side hadn't really been considered. One venture capitalist responded to my question about securing gigs quite cavalierly, saying, "We will just get all of the open job recs from Google." I didn't have the heart to tell him the consulting marketplace doesn't work that way.

Nonetheless, we discussed revenue models, intellectual property issues, contractual considerations, and privacy implications. The brainstorming was incredibly fun and made me appreciate that the Gig Economy world I had once known was evolving even further.

Those discussions prompted me to reconsider this on-demand consulting marketplace in which I had operated for so long. Marketplace platforms were being built at a rapid pace, but could their algorithms really displace strategic judgment? In my experience, one reason clients used an intermediary was to eliminate the noise that was coming from so many automated feeds and online resumes. Having M Squared say, "You should really talk to Mary, Harry, and Chris, and this is why" was a relief for so many overworked and stressed managers. Could a great algorithm really provide a similar level of comfort and thereby eliminate the humans in the process? If we really drive all business innovation through our people, isn't there some value to the people working the process by which we secure them? The very notion raises other questions, such as, as marketplaces proliferate, what would the consultants do: join all platforms or hedge their bets with the few that they like the best?

Additionally, I live in San Francisco, the home of the Uber mothership and its feisty competitor Lyft. A consequence of this is the never-ending stream of stories about the drive-sharing marketplace platforms and the ways these firms chose to treat their human partners, their drivers. All the discussions about whether Uber drivers should be employees or contractors seemed to drown out other segments of the Gig Economy. Stories about my old world, the high-end consultants and their experiences in the Gig Economy, seemed to be getting lost.

With that in mind, I decided to revisit the book I had written in 2001, *A New Brand of Expertise*. It focused on high-end independent consultants and the marketplace for their services. Beyond explaining what was then a new phenomenon, it offered guidance for companies that wanted to avail themselves of these services and best practices for the consultants pursuing the independent path. Although many of the business reasons for deploying on demand expertise have not changed, the landscape has. Due to this, the ways high-end gig workers need to establish their competency, market, and contract for services has changed. Similarly, companies can now access this expertise through many channels, so the internal vetting process becomes all the more important.

Moreover, companies must organize differently now to effectively deploy these gig workers. More importantly, they must empower their workforce in new ways, because not only are they engaging gig workers, they are preparing their own employees to become the gig workers of the future.

I was excited to revisit the subject, in part because I was no longer a player in the marketplace. Even though I was very even-handed with *A New Brand of Expertise*, it was still a promotional vehicle for my company, M Squared. Now, as the saying goes, I don't have a dog in the race, so my observations on the companies, business models, and industry developments can be far more candid. By extension, more people in the field were willing to speak to me because I was perceived to be independent.

And speak they did. To better understand these new dimensions of the Gig Economy world, I needed, in the words of Harry Truman, to learn the history I did not know. To do so, I interviewed a hearty cross-section of CEOs, COOs, and CTOs of new digital platform companies. I learned about new platforms that targeted highly specialized expertise, like cyber security experts or big data scientists. I spoke with specialty consulting firms that had narrowly defined talent offerings like social media influencers or experienced interim managers. I met with entrepreneurs developing adjacent systems to help companies better deploy consultants and manage the contractual and payment aspects of a workforce comprised of independent contractors as well as contract employees. Conversely, I met with entrepreneurs developing platforms to enable consultants to access and purchase the types of insurance coverages and retirement programs they will need in the new world of work. Finally, I met with pundits in the field to get their sense of where we stood in this movement, at the crest or in the trenches, to better understand the future world of work.

Beyond interviews, I also became a participant in the new Gig Economy. (Or, should I say, *more* of a participant, as by definition I am an "Occasional Independent," with some regular gigs and two paid board roles, as I will discuss more in Chapter 2.) I joined all of the digital platforms for which I was qualified and a few for which I probably was not, to get a sense of their process and communication with their community. I was deeply intrigued to see how many might produce gigs for me. Of the nine platforms I joined, three suggested opportunities for me. In only one case was the situation relevant to my background, which is an interesting data point, but just that: one point. As I explain in Chapter 5, you need to work the platforms for them to yield results, and after a while writing this book got in the way of that work.

I also became a client, using digital platforms to secure expertise for programming my personal website and market research services to capture data on different players in this new world of work. The programming project became somewhat of a nightmare, as I went through three different workers on two continents before I found one that could do the project as I intended. As that project finally progressed, the errors of the prior providers meant much more work was needed. I was not thrilled by that outcome, and neither was my new programmer, Phil, although it turned out to be a more lucrative gig for him. Being a client on the platform was instructive, at times surprising, and frequently frustrating, but helped to inform my perspective on the state of the art today.

As an aside, I even thought about becoming an Uber driver, but because I drive a Jaguar convertible, usually top down, that did not seem like a viable option.

Along the way, as I talked to friends and colleagues about the book, I became aware of a very important fact. Many people were clueless about the variety of business models in this new marketplace of talent. CEOs of companies that could really use a marketplace for big data geeks, for example, had no idea that such a site existed. The West Coast manager of a major consulting firm when we discussed some of my findings was relieved that someone was finally going to make sense of this new world of work. "I can only try," I replied.

The result is a book that I hope will provide insight into a very timely subject. In some ways, perhaps it is too timely. My first book, *A New Brand of Expertise*, had no chapter notes, and this book averages 10 per chapter. That is because every week, if not every day, new information was coming out about the Gig Economy. I started my research in January 2016. Since I began, there have been four books discussing elements of the phenomenon and 3 major industry studies, most notably the first comprehensive report on the topic by the McKinsey Global Institute. There were also five industry studies, including the annual *State of Independence in America* report from MBO Partners, a report that is well respected as a consistent source of data on the field, and a new study by the industry association, Staffing Industry Analysts, called *Measuring the Gig Economy*. At times I felt that I was drowning in data, so I did my best to make sense of it. This was no easy task, as all of the studies had their own methodologies, underlying assumptions, and associated results. I tried to glean the salient facts, the ones that could best educate my readers on the inner workings of the Gig Economy.

What I have put together is a well-researched but not academic perspective on how and why the new world of work, the Gig Economy, operates and grows. *Thriving in the Gig Economy* will hone in on the most important aspects of these trends and the implications for individuals and businesses. It will explain the digital talent marketplaces and how they fit into the talent landscape, outlining their features and cost structures.

Although not a how-to manual, *Thriving in the Gig Economy* will hopefully provide a clear explanation of how the participants in the Gig Economy, from workers to client companies to service providers, can succeed in the new marketplace. It begins with a definition of the Gig Economy to ensure that we are all on the same page (pardon the pun). From there, it discusses the people in the Gig Economy, their numbers, demographics, and motivations. A natural counterpart to that is why and how companies use these free agents, something workers need to understand to thrive. The book then compares traditional intermediaries and digital talent platforms, explaining how they differ and how individuals can best use these tools to their advantage. The book dives deep into personal branding including a broad discussion of building a digital voice. Although perhaps less interesting to many but just as important is the explanation of the legal issues surrounding this work mode as well as practical tips for managing your practice. The intent is to provide a framework for the reader to create his or her own mental model for how to thrive in the new world of work.

The structure of *Thriving in the Gig Economy* is designed to ensure that the reader gets real "take home" value from reading the book. Chapters on sales strategies, pricing, contract provisions, and creating the optimal independent work environment are designed to provide real assistance to existing gig workers as well as those who may be contemplating the idea. Similarly, I offer guidance on running a successful practice, provide a listing of popular freelancer apps, discuss ways to procure benefits, and offer insights into creating community as an independent worker. Each chapter concludes with a "Key Takeaways" section to underscore for the readers the points they need to understand in order to thrive.

And even though the discipline is constantly evolving, I had to offer some thoughts about what the future could hold. The short story is the trend will only continue and build, so the future looks bright. Nonetheless, there are many legal, regulatory, and societal issues that result from this growth that will need to be addressed in the years ahead. As is often said about Wayne Gretzky, he was a great hockey player because he anticipated where the puck would be. Hopefully my readers will become even more successful participants in the Gig Economy by anticipating the changes the future could bring.

It has been an adventure developing the content for this book. I have learned so much in the process of its development. I look forward to sharing it on the pages to come.

1

What Is the Gig Economy Anyway?

News about the Gig Economy is everywhere these days. The world seems to be awash in studies and initiatives aimed at this new world of work. Politicians are talking about it, as are journalists, businesspeople, and policy makers. Interestingly, the discussions don't always have a common thread. Here is a sampling of some recent headlines:

> "If you can't convince them, confuse them."
>
> —Harry S. Truman

"Skilled Professionals Will Dominate the Gig Economy, Report Says" (David Williams, *Small Business Trends,* 3/17/16)

"The Entire Online Gig Economy Might Be Mostly Uber" (Josh Zumbrun, *Wall Street Journal,* 3/28/16)

"Most Benefits of the Gig Economy Are Completely Imaginary" (Rebecca Smith, *Quartz,* 3/4/16)

"The Gig Economy Is Growing and It's Terrifying" (Hamilton Nolan, *Gawker,* 3/31/16)

"PWC Launches an Online Marketplace to Tap the Gig Economy" (*Financial Times,* 3/6/16)

Maybe it is just me, but it is hard to glean a common theme by perusing these news items all from the same month. On one hand, skilled professionals may make up the majority of the Gig Economy, but on the other, perhaps it is just comprised of Uber drivers after all. Any benefits may well be illusory, but obviously Price Waterhouse Coopers (PWC), the giant, well-respected, professional services firm, doesn't see it that way, and has invested not only its capital but also its brand in a digital talent marketplace. Nonetheless, despite the entry of premier firms like PWC, the future of the Gig Economy is scary. The contradictions go on and on. So what is the truth?

As Oscar Wilde said, "the truth is rarely pure and never simple." And that would be the case here. Part of the problem is language; not only does the Gig Economy mean different things to different people, the very word *gig* does as well. So without a common vocabulary and therefore a common starting point, confusion reigns. There are also adjacent issues, such as all of the technology platforms pursuing this space, the absence of benefits or a social safety net for many participants, and the resulting emotion arising from the social impact of the movement. Taken in its entirety, the topic can seem overwhelming. It's not, so let's dial it back and get on the same page.

The Gig Economy Defined

Let's start at the beginning and develop a common understanding of what the Gig Economy is and what it is not. Dictionary.com offers as its fourth definition of the word "gig"—behind a two-wheel carriage, a fishing hook, and a military demerit—the following:

1. A single professional engagement, usually of short duration, as of jazz or rock musicians.

2. Any job, especially one of short or uncertain duration.[1]

The first reference became widely used in the 1920s as jazz became more popular in America. Musicians would refer to the work they would secure with a band, whether for one night or for one month, as a "gig." Similarly, someone who moonlighted as a musician might refer to the work as a "side gig."

Other uses of *gig* began to emerge, especially during the Depression, as companies hired day laborers. Rebecca Smith, the deputy director of the National Employment Law Project, points out that today's big Gig Economy companies, like Uber and Instacart, all talk as if they are different from old-style employers simply because they operate online. "But in fact," she says, "they are operating just like farm labor contractors, garment jobbers and day labor centers of old."[2] Similarly, as the World Economic Forum Report just noted "although digital formats for connecting people to work are new, the act of ad-hoc work or self-employment is not."[3]

AND WHILE WE'RE AT IT, LET'S TALK ABOUT JOBS

As we discuss the origin of the term *gig*, let's not forget that our current understanding of the word *job* is a very recent, post-Depression construct. Again, if you go back to the dictionary, there are many of definitions for a job. The first that appears in the Oxford English Dictionary is "a piece of work" done as part of one's regular work or profession. Several variations follow, including my personal favorite: a criminal enterprise, i.e., "they did the bank job." There is also the cosmetic surgery spin of a "nose job." Regular remunerative employment, how most people think of a job today, is well down the list. One last interesting tidbit: The medieval origins of *job* are thought to be from a word that means a lump of dung. Ironic, isn't it?

The extension of the gig concept to any job including highly skilled ones began to build in the 1980s. The corporate consolidations in the 1980s redefined the employment landscape. In the latter half of the next decade, the number of firms falling off the *Fortune* 500 list reached new heights, as the earlier decade's merger and acquisition activity led to massive restructuring of bloated organizations ravaged by inflation and international competition. Layoffs came to be known as downsizing and then, even more euphemistically, rightsizing. These staff reductions combined with the adoption of new "just in time" management philosophies resulted in the elimination of many managerial roles. This launched the first wave of modern freelance businesspeople.

Freelancers had long been a staple in the creative industry; advertising creative directors built their reputations on the stable of freelancers they controlled, whether they were copywriters, illustrators, or photographers.

The movie industry, too, had been a freelance marketplace, since the 1940s. From its origins in the 1920s, it was vertically integrated; actors, directors, writers, and technical staff worked for the studios, and the studios owned the cinemas. The time period, referred to as either the studio system years or the Golden Age of Hollywood, was known for formula movies, with actors playing very similar roles in similar stories, because the business formula was to utilize the talent that was on the payroll at the studio. (Think about all those old Fred Astaire and Ginger Rogers movies.) The change came in 1948 when a Supreme Court ruling required the studios to divest themselves of their distribution operations. At the same time, a threat appeared from another corner, as technological advances resulted in a new media form: television.

As the studio system broke down, the talent began to take control of their own careers. Talent agencies emerged as the market makers in talent, and unions arose to protect various specialties. In fact, many have pointed to this parallel as a reason why Gig Economy workers may need to unionize. In the movie business today, people come together in all the disciplines (writers, actors, set designers, assistant directors and key grips, to name just a few) to create a film. Once it is over, the various players disband and go on to the next gig.

Gig work in the mainstream business world evolved a bit more slowly. It wasn't until the 1980s that independent consultants in core business functional areas, such as finance, marketing, and human resources, began "hanging out their own shingles" or going into business for themselves in large numbers. In the next decade, as technology changed business communications and enhanced mobility, the trend accelerated.

Other factors drove this entrepreneurial development as well. In 1989, Felice Schwartz of Catalyst, a national organization focused on helping women chose and manage professional careers, published the now-famous "Mommy Track" article, in which she revised the notion of the glass ceiling for women in corporate positions. She pointed out that maternity leaves and family obligations impaired the upward mobility of women in corporate America. That said, many women were opting for a different future, one in which they could marry their professional expertise and their need for flexibility in their personal lives. Credentialed women with advanced degrees and strong business experience became consultants to gain control over their lives.

Similarly, others became consultants because they wanted to write the great American novel, build furniture, or write music; consulting enabled them to fund what might be a less lucrative but more rewarding creative pursuit. For example, one of our top consultants at M Squared had been the head of international human resources for one of the largest banks in the world, but his passion was sculpting. Being a sculptor is a dirty profession, so he wanted a more flexible professional lifestyle in which he could spend entire days not in an office. On those days, he could also pursue his passion and not worry about all of the marble dust.

Firms emerged to create a market to match the buyers, companies, with the sellers, the consultants. My firm, M Squared Consulting, was one of those early pioneers, and frankly the marketplace did not know what to make of us. We had a network of independent consultants that we matched to projects to help clients meet their business needs. (We had this network before the Internet, I might add, but I am dating myself.) On the one hand, we were like staffing firms, but our people had higher billing rates. On the other hand, our services were akin to executive search firms, because we were locating very specific expertise, but the roles our consultants filled were temporary. Then again, we were also like consulting firms, because we handled the same type of high-level problems and bid on the same projects as brand name consulting firms, like McKinsey or Accenture. We were a hybrid service in a nascent market that was ready to take off. Because this was a high-value service, an intermediary to facilitate the process made economic sense for all involved; getting just the right expertise for a high-profile, mission-critical gig was worth the cost.

During the last 10 years, the market has changed dramatically as new technologies enabled the development of large-scale marketplaces for relatively low-value services. Now, with the ubiquity of mobile communications, the proliferation of apps, and America's impatient 24/7 way of life in most urban centers, identifying someone who could make your life more convenient, by delivering your groceries via Instacart or getting you where you need to be through Uber, became worth a price. This convenience dimension is what most people refer to as the On-Demand Economy. Investors determined that this convenience factor had sufficient volume so that even though these new firms offered a relatively low value service, money could still be made.

In Chapter 2, we will explore more about who these gig workers are, but for now, let's agree that **a *gig* is a job of uncertain duration in any field, whether it's a driver, a freelance artist, or an interim CEO.** "Gigs" are what has historically been called contingent work, whether it is secured by the worker, through a staffing company, through a human capital company, or through a digital talent platform. The *Gig Economy,* then, refers to the companies and business systems that have evolved to support this independent work.

The On-Demand Economy

The On-Demand Economy is a subset of the larger Gig Economy and refers to economic activities that arise from digital marketplaces that fulfill customer needs through "immediate" access to goods and services. Immediate is noteworthy here, as that is a relative term. My need for transportation now means that I want my Uber driver to arrive as soon as possible. In fact, a half hour would be a long time to wait. That said, I may have an immediate need for an interim CFO, but I do not expect to see that person on my doorstep (truthfully, that could be a bit disconcerting), but finding them in a day or two would be tremendous. Immediacy, then, is conditioned by the skill set I am seeking.

That skill set also adds other parameters to the decision. I don't care who picks up my dry cleaning through TaskRabbit, but I do care who steps into run my marketing department while my manager is on maternity leave. So, an additional consideration is the duration of my need. Similarly, anyone can put up with even the chattiest Lyft driver for a short trip, but if I need a project manager for six months, I want to have a better sense of the individual filling that role. The chemistry or fit of the individual becomes more of a factor.

One could make the argument that the difference in immediacy is whether the customer is a business or an individual; immediacy has a shorter half-life in the B2C (business-to-consumer) market than it does in the B2B (business-to-business) market. That said, there are some individuals who buy services from marketplaces such as Upwork, a digital marketplace for programmers and creative freelancers, or the Gerson Lehman Group, an expertise platform. This author, for example, contracted for certain industry research from an expert procured on Zintro. In fact, 26 percent of Gig Economy workers spent $101 billion in 2015 hiring other independent workers.[4] The following chart gives a sense of where different business models fall in this immediacy framework.

The Immediacy Map
The more urgent and short-term the need, the less skill is required

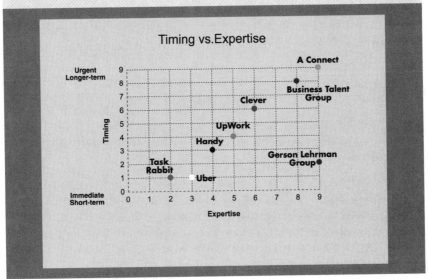

One key aspect of the new On-Demand world is that it is based on a technology platform, and the platform handles the settlement of the financial transaction. At the higher end of the skill spectrum, the platforms are built with algorithms designed to match the precise expertise needed for the client with the requisite experience of the individual. The algorithms improve as more successful matches are made, and as such, there is a first mover value; the firm that can capture the largest number of projects at the start will be further along in perfecting its algorithm. (We will discuss the talent platform world in more detail in Chapter 6.)

The economics of the On-Demand world dictate that the shorter the time frame, the lower the fee, and similarly, the more commoditized the expertise, the lower the fee. As such, the platforms in the lower left of the preceding chart are predicated on highly efficient operations and high volumes. They also benefit from the network effect: the more people in the network, both users and gig workers, the more volume is generated, and the higher the value of that network.

These firms in the lower left also have the largest challenge from an employment law standpoint. The tasks performed are low skilled. Most players started with the lowest cost business model, calling their gig workers independent contractors (ICs) rather than employees. Legally, ICs, because they are not employees, do not get the benefits typically accorded to employees such as payment of statutory payroll taxes, paid time off, access to healthcare, and retirement programs. These costs for the employer are estimated at 32 to 37 percent of payroll costs. It is no surprise, then, that many on-demand companies started with the idea that their workers could be ICs.

Alternatively, employees need to be managed by strict wage and hour regulations, so there is a level of inflexibility to these roles. A hallmark of the on-demand service world was that the workers could set their own schedules. As such, the reasoning went, the workers shouldn't be viewed as employees.

Unfortunately, this area of the law is ambiguous at best, because "independent contractor" (IC) is an undefined term in the law. (See Chapter 7 for more on this subject.) Because there is no legal definition of an IC, tests have been developed that take into account agency law as well as other factors. The IRS has put the most widely used framework together in its "20 Points" that define an independent contractor. These include things like having their own tools, being able to experience a financial loss, and receiving no training. Unfortunately, not all of the conditions need to be met, and some are more important than others. This makes for a very murky picture of what constitutes an IC versus an employee. In the last 20 years, the two key things that businesses have drawn from the "20 Points" are that the most important considerations are direction and control of the enterprise over the individual; if you direct and/or control the work of someone, they are likely your employee.

Many on-demand service companies are changing the way in which they treat their gig workers. Eden, a grocery delivery service, decided it wanted to have more control over its employees to improve customer satisfaction. Munchery, a prepared food delivery service, needed to be able to exercise more control over schedules and thus employees to ensure on-time deliveries. Similarly, valet parking service Luxe needed the power to assign its valets to certain locations to ensure coverage. Control was key in all three cases. These business model changes could have occurred for any number of reasons, but it is hard to imagine that staving off a government employment lawsuit was not one of them. Witness another firm that did not change its model. Homejoy, a house cleaning service, backed with $40 million in venture capital, did not make the call soon enough and ended up closing its doors in 2015 in large part due to worker misclassification issues.

Washington is taking notice of all this activity. The Department of Labor (DOL), acting in a way that, in hindsight, seems foolhardy, stopped its regular reporting on the contingent economy in 2005. It announced in January 2016 that the DOL will be reinstating that study in May 2017. Different politicians are calling for increased scrutiny and potentially regulation of the employment practices of the On-Demand Economy. Elizabeth Warren, speaking about these employment issues, recently said:

The gig economy didn't invent any of these problems. In fact, the gig economy has become a stopgap for some workers who can't make ends meet in a weak labor market. The much-touted virtues of flexibility, independence, and creativity offered by gig work might be true for some workers under some conditions, but for many, the gig economy is simply the next step in a losing effort to build some economic security in a world where all the benefits are floating to the top 10%.[5]

(We will discuss what this means for you and your business in more depth in Chapter 10.)

PROFILE: CLEVER

Cat Lincoln had a 20-year career in marketing when she started to work with influencers on a new form of word-of-mouth marketing. Called influencer marketing, this new approach, a natural extension of a brand's marketing or PR initiatives, uses bloggers, Instagrammers, YouTubers, and more to tell authentic brand stories. Cat's business model was to create a network of paid, professional social media influencers, a cohort known to be disparate and highly independent, but increasingly trusted by their communities.

With thousands of influencers—from pets to professional athletes—in its network, CLEVER puts together custom programs for Fortune 500 companies. The influencer marketing industry was originally powered by "mommy bloggers" and has now grown to be a key marketing approach in the food, fashion, beauty, sports, tech, and DIY markets. CLEVER is the industry leader.

Influencers are usually paid per program and can earn anywhere from $50 to $100 to share a piece of content, to tens of thousands of dollars for a more complicated "ask" such as creating an original product video. For professional social media influencers with established followings, CLEVER provides another source of gig income.

The Sharing Economy

Another important term to understand as we set the stage for *Thriving in the Gig Economy* is the Sharing Economy. Although it is often used interchangeably with the Gig Economy, it is not a synonym. The Sharing Economy refers to the economic activity generated from the sharing of physical assets on a peer-to-peer level. The poster child for the sharing economy is AirBnB, the home-sharing service, that enables individuals to rent their property or a portion of it to people in need of a vacation rental. Although the host may need to prepare the house for the guest, that is not the service that is being purchased; the vacationer is buying a room for the night, not a turn-down service delivered by the owner. As such, the product is the temporary housing.

Other assets can be involved in the Sharing Economy as well. There are several peer-to-peer lending platforms, like Lending Club, in which individuals can pool financial assets and make loans to individuals or enterprises in need of funds. Share a Mortgage is a London-based startup that allows individuals to pool resources for the purchase of real property. eBay is also a sharing platform, allowing individuals to sell handicrafts or Grandma's antique dining room set.

It is worth mentioning that there is some intersection with the Gig Economy when the asset being shared is in part intangible. For example, SofaConcerts in Hamburg, Germany, allows people to host musicians in their home for paying guests. The home is being shared, but the experience—the performance—is also shared. Similarly, EatWith in San Francisco allows hosts to open their homes to put on a dinner party for groups of interesting strangers. The home and meal are shared, but the host has done the work to prepare the meal. The host could be an expert chef, so in that sense expertise is being purchased.

That said, the key distinction between the Sharing Economy and the Gig Economy is that the former involves the purchase of a service or experience that involves a physical asset, whereas the latter is a time-bound, personally delivered service. At the high value end of the Gig Economy, the transaction can include an intangible asset, like the intellectual property that is developed on the gig. A physical asset isn't involved. Similarly, the Sharing Economy can intersect with the On-Demand Economy if the value proposition of the service being procured involves some urgency. If I need to board my dog tomorrow, DogVacay, where people take care of pets for discrete time periods, is a platform through which I can procure that service on demand.

As an aside, one aspect of the sharing economy is that many people, from entrepreneurs to policy makers, have looked toward this economic structure in the interest of reducing waste through better asset utilization. Why build more cars when so many cars are sitting in garages? The founder of BlaBla Car, a French firm that rents spaces in cars with empty seats for long-term trips, said that "the initial motivation was the waste, the unbearable waste that empty cars on the road represent."[6] The consignment platform ThreadUp touts that by using the platform to recycle clothing or acquire gently worn items, you are reducing your carbon footprint and reducing waste.

The Sharing Economy, the On-Demand Economy, and the digital talent marketplaces are based on technology platforms and share the feature of handling the financial settlement of the transactions online. Staffing Industry Analysts, one of the foremost experts in the study of work, has defined talent platform arrangements, in which the entire life of the transaction, from sourcing the work to paying for it, is totally online as the Human Cloud.[7]

This common financial attribute was central to a study the JP Morgan Chase Institute conducted in 2015 on income volatility. This is the first study to use big data to try to get a sense of the impact of the new technology platforms. The Chase research team looked at deposits in accounts of 260,000 customers and distinguished between primary employment income and supplementary income from digital platforms. They defined labor platforms as the on-demand gig companies such as Uber and TaskRabbit, and capital platforms such as eBay and AirBnB. The researchers found that the platforms differed from each other in terms of who used them, how frequently, and what percentage of earnings they represented for the individual.[8] (We will go into greater detail about these distinctions in the next chapter.)

One could argue that Uber and Lyft, the ride-sharing services, can be seen as the trifecta, because they check the boxes that qualify them for each of these different economic frameworks. The driver owns the asset (the car), that is involved in the transaction, so this is a Sharing Economy service. The driver also uses his or her licensed driving expertise to perform the chauffeuring function, which is temporary and of uncertain duration, so it can be considered a gig. Additionally, that service is typically urgent, so it is part of the On-Demand Economy as well. Similarly, the app handles the financial element of the transaction.

In summary, these terms, which are widely used interchangeably, are all related yet slightly different. There is an intersection for many firms and functions. There are common processes, but the distinctions arising from tangible or intangible assets, expertise levels, and urgency are important to consider.

The New Economies

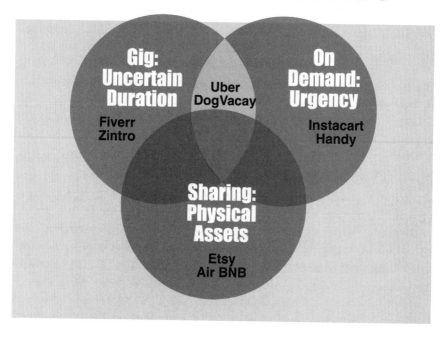

Finally, although the Gig Economy is regularly in the news, it is still a new phenomenon for many Americans. A recent Pew Research study indicates that 89 percent of Americans were unaware of the Gig Economy. "Exposure to these shared, collaborative and on-demand services at a broad level is heavily concentrated among certain demographic cohorts," according to Pew.[9] My interpretation of this remark is that the Gig Economy was narrowly defined around the digital platform world. Other research has consistently shown that, although adoption is growing, the number of participants is very small compared to the overall workforce.

However, other statistics suggest that the Gig Economy may be more far-reaching. Recent studies, which we will discuss more in Chapter 2, have estimated that the Gig Economy includes 44 million independent workers.[10] Another 29 million people are considering becoming independent workers in the near term.[11] Those more than 70 million people would represent about 21 percent of the United States economy, making the Pew study numbers a bit curious.

It could well be that a certain proportion of these workers do not see themselves as part of the Gig Economy. As I said earlier, it could be that the research was really focused on the Sharing Economy and On-Demand Economy. As such, other independent workers who don't utilize those platforms may not have been included. Perhaps the research authors did not appreciate the nuanced difference between the terms. They didn't have the advantage of reading this book.

Chapter 1 Key Takeaways

- The Gig Economy refers to the economic value derived from the increasing trend of people working in jobs of indefinite duration, which, unlike traditional employment, are finite in nature.

- The On-Demand Economy is a subset of the Gig Economy and refers to the economic activity from digital marketplaces that deliver goods or services when invoked.

- A key distinction between the On-Demand Economy and the Gig Economy is the immediacy of the need, where immediacy depends on the requisite skill level and duration of the gig.

- The Sharing Economy refers to the economic activity from peer-to-peer transactions in which a physical asset is involved in the delivery of a good or service.

- The Sharing Economy and the On-Demand Economy involve technology platforms that also handle the financial settlement of the transaction.

2

Sizing the Gig Economy:
The Lay of the Land

Popular culture is often a great lens through which to observe societal change. When I was growing up in the '60s, the Cleavers from *Leave it to Beaver* were the quintessential TV family. Ward, a busy executive (at where, we never quite knew), epitomized the "company man," while June maintained the household, wearing pearls and an apron as she looked after Wally and the "Beaver." Ward's work was steady, and you knew he would someday retire with a pension and gold watch, a reward for his years of able service. Compare that to today, where *Modern Family* tops the ratings. Jay Pritchett is a small business owner, Phil Dunphy is a real estate agent and therefore an independent contractor, and Cameron Tucker is a stay-at-home dad who plays drum gigs on the side. Not a gold watch in sight....

> "The strange truth is, if you ave a so-called proper full-time job today, you are in the minority. The world has changed and few have noticed."
>
> —Charles Handy, *The Second Curve*

It is interesting to see how completely the company man image has faded from view. Whereas 20 years ago new entrants into the business world hoped for a job for the long term, now conventional wisdom among the Millennial generation, those born in the 1980s through 2000, is that 18 months to a year is about the right time to stay at a first job. The corporate ladder many of us fully intended to climb back in the day has now become a ladder for some, but more of a step stool for most.

Implications of the Corporate Step Stool

There are many reasons why we are seeing increased mobility in the workplace. The corporate layoffs and dislocations of the 1980s and 1990s accelerated the erosion of the social contract implicit in the company man myth. The high-profile bankruptcy of Enron in 2001, which vaporized the pensions of so many employees, only reinforced the belief that corporate employers were not always dependable. Long-term security was a thing of the past. Because such security was a key factor in job loyalty, loyalty waned.

This pattern has continued. A recent study surveyed the attitudes of independent workers. It showed that the Gen Xers, ages 37–51, were the demographic group that bore the brunt of the 8.7 million jobs lost in the recession of 2008–2010. Many of those became independent workers. In the annual study of independent work by MBO Partners, an employment platform, 47 percent of the independent workers in this age group felt that their prior employer did not understand their value, and this was a factor contributing to their decision to become independent.[1]

So rather than climb the ladder, many professionally displaced businesspeople sought to take back control of their lives and launched independent consulting careers. In this way, the loss of one client doesn't result in the loss of all of your earnings. Similarly, your future role and earnings potential are not dependent on the decisions made by someone at corporate headquarters miles away. Independence has its risks, but it also has its own rewards, such as security. For some, that is counterintuitive, but being in control of one's destiny is a key driver for most independent workers.

Technology has also played a part in the explosive growth of independent consulting. It used to be that when you came to an employer, you spent several months learning the internal systems, highly customized programs, and the attendant procedures that drove the business. It was important to understand "the way we do things here." As such, the development of that informal and formal system knowledge became a valuable skill set for the employee to move within the organization as well as an asset for the organization, who needed adept employees steeped in their arcane processes and systems.

In the last decade, though, more and more businesses have moved operations to the cloud and standardized their office infrastructures around popular platforms like Gmail for email communications or Salesforce for contact management. They may still have sophisticated, customized special purpose systems, but "the way we do things here" is no longer so much of a mystery. New hires can come in knowing Salesforce, and that platform knowledge makes them more interesting to the employer and, at the same time, more mobile. As such, they now have far more step ladders from which to choose—ladders they may ascend as an employee, a consultant, or a free agent.

Similarly, the emergence of talent matching platforms like Upwork and Hourly Nerd (recently renamed Catalant) has hastened the freelancing trend. Behavioral economist Richard Thaler posited in his book, *Nudge,* that people are more likely to make choices when the options appear to be easy. Thirty years ago, you had to be very confident not only in your subject matter expertise, but also in your own ability to sell yourself, if you decided to create an independent consulting career. Now, with the increasing presence of digital matching sites, the decision is much easier. Aside from the most specialized, applying to these networks is simple, often requiring just a LinkedIn profile. That simplicity gives some workers the nudge they need to consider the freelance opportunity, accelerating the supply side of the equation.

Another thing that has helped "nudge" people toward independent life has been the passage of the Affordable Care Act (ACA). When I wrote my first book in 2001, access to health insurance benefits was a constraint, forcing some people to abandon the independent life and cycle back to employment. Jody Miller, CEO of the Business Talent Group, sees the ACA as important driver in the continued growth of the independent worker trend. (We will discuss what potential changes to the ACA may mean for the marketplace in Chapter 10.)

ADVENTURES IN APPLICATIONS

As part of this book project, I applied to many digital matching sites to better understand their process and their human, not just their graphical, interface. In the spring of 2016, I applied to Hourly Nerd, now called Catalant, which touts MBA consultants from prestigious business schools. It vets its consultants in part through their email addresses; they ask applicants to use their business school–assigned email accounts. Although my alma mater, the Haas School at UC Berkeley, was among the elite, I could not register, because I graduated before the advent of email. I contacted the site, explaining that when I went to business school, email had not yet been invented. I knew that they did not want to discriminate against older MBAs, so I wondered how else I might apply. I was accepted the next day, with an email that said, *"Although we require that consultants sign up using their school specific email address, we have waived this requirement for your convenience."* My conclusion was that either no one in the management team is older than 40 or very few senior consultants have signed on to the platforms, or they would have anticipated my issue. Interestingly, in November, when my daughter applied, the business school email was no longer a requirement.

Additionally, digital talent platforms help eliminate a barrier to deploying freelance professional expertise, which is trust. Arun Sundararajan in his recent book, *The Sharing Economy: The End of Employment and the Rise of Crowd Based Capitalism,* points to the importance of the digitization of trust in the adoption of new platform technologies.[2] From our experiences with longer-lived platforms like eBay or TripAdvisor, we have come to trust people and firms we do not know by relying on the feedback that has been provided about them by other patrons who have shared their feedback online. Just like you rate your Uber driver after every trip, in the professional services world, clients of contractors are asked to rate the services they received from a platform participant. Indeed, for many users, these rating systems become a vendor and/or product selection screen; they limit the set of Amazon sellers they patronize to those with the highest ratings. By increasing trust, the rating system is intended to increase adoption on the demand side. It is safe for me to hire this consultant, sight unseen, because she has done good work for someone else.

So the step ladders may be shorter, but there are far more of them. Just to be clear, the traditional work model, in which an individual provides services for a company where he or she is an employee, continues to be the most prevalent model, and is unlikely to disappear any time soon. At the same time, though, alternative work arrangements provide other benefits to the participants in terms of control, flexibility, and variety and are growing in use throughout the world. In fact, a 2016 McKinsey Global Institute(MGI) study found that there are nearly 87 million people in the United States and Europe who would prefer to pursue an independent lifestyle.[3]

A Word on Independent Worker Data

At this point, I need to explain the data problem around the independent workforce. The U.S. government stopped its contingent labor survey in 2005, so there are no government statistics available. Efforts have been made to try to estimate the independent workforce from 1099 data and/or self-employment data, but both approaches are problematic. In the case of 1099 data, for example, the data could include dividends income in addition to non-W2 work-related income. Private sources, from industry players to think tanks, have also done research in this area, and their results present very different estimates of the scale and size of the independent workforce. In fact, the MGI report listed five different studies, including its own, that estimated the size of the independent workforce in the United States as a percentage of the working population. The results were broad, ranging from as little as 16 percent to as high as 27 percent.[4] This comparison did not include the Staffing Industry Analysts (SIA) report, which suggests independent workers account for 29 percent of the U.S. working population, which would broaden that range even further.

Suffice it to say, there are many different numbers published about the Gig Economy, and it is difficult to determine which is the most accurate or relevant, as different methodologies and assumptions underlie the results. As such, I will cite my sources when offering numbers, but recognize there are many studies, which look at this workforce in slightly different ways.

The Independent Worker Defined

Contingent workers are defined by the Bureau of Labor Statistics as those "who do not have an explicit or implicit contract for long-term employment."[5] Interestingly, *long-term* is not defined, but a good rule of thumb is more than one year. That said, there are long-term contract or consulting situations that can extend more than a year. As part of my research, I conducted a survey of independent consultants and asked them if they felt they were part of the Gig Economy. One respondent said he was not because his contracts typically were longer than a year. I would disagree, by the way, and suggest that as an independent worker, he is still a part of the Gig Economy, even if he happens to have long gigs.

(As an aside, I ran my "Consulting in the Gig Economy" Survey in November 2016. Respondents came from several channels: M Squared invited its network, the consulting group on LinkedIn was sent a link, and visitors to my blog could also respond. Participants were anonymous, so I cannot offer attribution for comments. There were 97 respondents.)

These independent workers secure their engagements through any number of channels. The recent Staffing Industry Analysts (SIA) report defined the channels in the following way[6]:

- An independent contractor providing services to a company; these individuals are typically self-employed and cover a wide variety of occupations, many of them high level. (**Consulting/ ICs**)

- An employee of a contracting or consulting firm who provides project-based services to a company; these individuals operate on a Statement of Work (SOW) basis, and although they are employees of the consulting firm, work directly with a client. (We will discuss Statements of Work in more detail in Chapter 5.) (**SOW Contracting**)

- An employee of a temporary staffing service; these individuals take on assignments that range from clerical roles to professional and managerial ones. (**Staffing**)

- A worker who secured work through a digital talent platform; these include talent platforms such as Uber or Upwork. They do not include product-based platforms such as Etsy or AirBnB. (**Human Cloud**)

- Temporary workers who are directly sourced by clients. These include roles like substitute teachers who are employed by school districts on an as-needed basis or seasonal retail hires. **(Direct Temporary)**

Independent Workforce Channels

Consulting/ ICs
23.5 Million Workers

15.3% of US Workforce

SOW Contracting
2.9 Million Workers

1.9% of US Workforce

Staffing
9.5 Million Workers

6.2% of US Workforce

Human Cloud
9.7 Million Workers

6.6% of US Workforce

Direct Temporary
5.5 Million Workers

3.6% of US Workforce

TOTAL IN 2015

44.1 Million Workers

29% of US Workforce

Source: Staffing Industry Analysts

It is important to note that in the consulting category, a project could have come via the individual's own sales effort or through an intermediary, such as the Business Talent Group. I distinguish between two specific types of intermediaries—specialty consulting firms and digital platforms—because their business models are fundamentally different.

Specialty Consulting Firms and Digital Marketplaces

Specialty consulting firms, like my old firm, M Squared, achieve results by brokering independent consultants. They may be highly automated and may have a sophisticated technology infrastructure, but they typically facilitate the matching process with some degree of human expertise. At a more granular level, they may take responsibility for the work product and may employ the consultants for the duration of the engagement. They are also key participants in the Statement of Work segment, facilitating this SOW-based consulting for their network of independent workers. Most importantly, these firms consider themselves consulting or human capital firms, not technology companies. Their brand promise is providing solutions. Moreover, its brand and reputation are key to consultants becoming part of the network. In my consulting survey, 47 percent of respondents ranked the reputation of the firm as a reason for affiliation. This makes sense; if M Squared has a great reputation in the technology sector and you work for tech companies, you will want to become part of the M Squared network. Per Chris Neal, a former consultant who now works as a principal at M Squared overseeing solution delivery, "It's not the horse that matters, it's the jockey."[7]

Conversely, talent matching firms, such as Upwork or Fiverr, define themselves as technology companies. In fact, the CEO of Fiverr, Micha Kaufman, noted on the Future of Work podcast that Fiverr was in fact a technology company, modeled after Amazon, to allow consumers to browse and buy skill sets.[8] These firms match skill sets through algorithms, and their business model is all about expanding the platform and perfecting their algorithmic accuracy. Although increasing sales is important, the growth they seek comes from selling the platform to other marketplaces. Their brand promise is providing the best match with the best algorithm.

It is hard to say how many people are actually working through digital talent platforms. The U.S. Department of Commerce recently released a study in which it defines companies in this segment as "digital matching firms."[9] In addition to the data problems I noted earlier, this study explained that data about the numbers of workers is unreliable, in part because many of these digital matching platforms are privately held companies and don't want to release proprietary data about their operations. The MGI report stated that only 8 percent of those surveyed who offered independent labor services had used a digital platform to secure work.[10]

Another recent study undertaken by PYMNTS.com and Hyperwallet, entitled Gig Economy Index, focused on the digital platform market only. In fact, they appropriated the Gig Economy term to be defined very narrowly to include only work secured on digital platforms or in the human cloud. This study and its findings differed greatly from the other published studies. This was due in part to its survey structure sampling methodology. To ensure a technology-savvy sample, researchers surveyed more than 3,400 shoppers who had made purchases using a mobile device.[11] According to Nielsen, a leading demographic and trend marketing firm, age matters when considering mobile buying patterns. Millennials, those ages 21–34, make up 50 percent of mobile purchasers.[12] As such, the sample most likely skewed young and highlighted the behaviors and characteristics of a younger cohort. They extrapolated based on smartphone usage, that 90.2 million people found work on gig platforms, which would be 28 percent of the U.S. workforce. Given that this result is such an outlier compared to other studies, I won't be using this report, but I mention it to highlight the great deal of noise that surrounds the digital talent marketplace.

As skill sets become more senior and specialized, the business model of the more professionally oriented digital matching sites changes, placing a far greater emphasis on vetting candidates. UpCounsel, a legal marketplace, only accepted 400 attorneys from 10,000 applicants. Similarly, Experfy, a data scientist marketplace, accepted 3,300 from more than 20,000 applicants. In order to offer the curated platform of highly specialized talent, more emphasis must be put on the vetting the network. (We will discuss these platforms and their processes in more detail in Chapter 6.)

Additionally, for independent workers operating at these more senior and accomplished levels, the competition for projects changes as well, because the product is no longer a commodity offering. Some of these platforms will compete against the human capital companies and certain high-end staffing firms, because these firms are brokers of senior-level talent. And, of course, at the senior professional level, all of the players in the market compete against the freelancer himself; based on her expertise, she can secure a prime project on her own by virtue of reputation, referrals, and past clients.

The overall marketplace for expertise can be viewed as a pyramid. There are a myriad of digital platforms at the base along with staffing companies offering low-skill, low-dollar commoditized opportunities.

The next rung incorporates a bit more skill and more specialization, with platforms for drivers, entertainers, telecomm workers, and copywriters. Competition here comes from specialty staffing firms and at times the freelancer himself. At the upper echelon are the high-paying gigs. The digital matching sites are fewer and include some highly specialized players. Specialty consulting firms also enter the mix. Most importantly though, the freelancer, because of his valuable expertise, is both a resource to these firms and a competitor.

The Expertise Pyramid

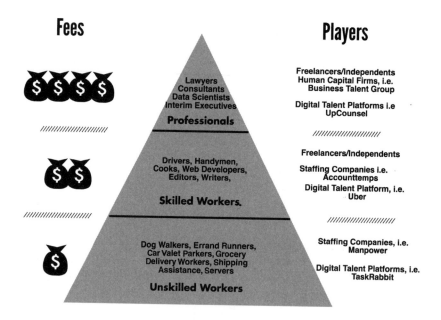

Fees

Players

**Lawyers
Consultants
Data Scientists
Interim Executives**

Professionals

Freelancers/Independents
Human Capital Firms, i.e.
Business Talent Group

Digital Talent Platforms i.e
UpCounsel

**Drivers, Handymen,
Cooks, Web Developers,
Editors, Writers,**

Skilled Workers.

Freelancers/Independents

Staffing Companies i.e.
Accounttemps
Digital Talent Platform, i.e.
Uber

**Dog Walkers, Errand Runners,
Car Valet Parkers, Grocery
Delivery Workers, Shipping
Assistance, Servers**

Unskilled Workers

Staffing Companies, i.e.
Manpower

Digital Talent Platforms, i.e.
TaskRabbit

The Top of the Pyramid

The upper portion of the pyramid represents significant profit potential in the Gig Economy. Individuals need to work their way to the upper portion by developing a body of work and perhaps earning advanced degrees that can enable them to command higher fees. So who are the people that are making money in the gig world? Today's gig worker may be a freelancer, independent consultant, independent contractor, or specialist. I will use the terms interchangeably going forward.

MBO partners is a specialized staffing company that has served the independent contractor community for decades. They were one of the pioneers in providing employment options and specialty services for independent workers to help them manage their practices more effectively. They have also been thought leaders in the field, conducting one of the only regular surveys of independent workers. The value of their report is its consistency and comparability year-to-year.

The 6th Annual MBO Partners State of Independence study published in 2016 reported[13]:

- The independent expertise marketplace is expected to grow 16.4 percent over the next five years.

- This market now numbers 39.8 million people. (Keep in mind this refers to their definition of independent worker but is in the same general vicinity as the SI report quoted earlier.)

- These freelance workers generated more than $1.1 trillion revenue in 2015, representing 6 percent of U.S. GDP.

Each year, the MBO Partners study segments the market by career importance and looks at full-time independents, part-time independents, and occasional independents. Here are some interesting facts about the segments:

- Full-time independents are those who work more than 15 hours per week, and two-thirds of those work more than 35 hours per week. They number 16.9 million, which is a drop from the 2015 report. The authors surmise that the economic recovery led some independents to return to regular employment. Many independents describe having a portfolio career, in which they will move in and out of independent consulting and employment. As one consultant once said to me, "It's just a 2-year gig."

Nearly half of the full-time independents report that they make more money on their own than they had as an employee. Sixteen percent, or 2.9 million, earn more than $100K. This high-earning group has been growing at 7.7 percent each year, with earnings averaging $192K.

- Part-time independents work between one and 15 hours per week. These number about 12.4 million people, and they are pursuing gigs as a way to make more money on the side. Almost three-quarters have other jobs that may be largely full-time, which is why they have fewer hours to work on gigs. This group also includes retirees, who may prefer a lighter workload. For some, the part-time gig is a backup, if something were to go wrong with the full-time job. This "lifeboat" notion may relate back to the lack of faith in traditional organizations to provide security.

- Occasional independents are those who pursue freelancing when in need of extra cash. Informally, I poll every Uber driver I encounter, and this occasional independent seems to be a high proportion of the driver mix in my unscientific survey. I have had massage therapists, teachers, and retirees who drive to pocket extra cash. Perhaps most interesting was a fellow who was making a living on fantasy football winnings and driving for Uber to socialize. Although this cohort encompasses all age groups, Millennials, those born between 1980 and 2000, are a natural fit here. These ranks are estimated at 10.5 million in 2016. This segment also had a slight reduction from the 2015 numbers.

The MGI study looked at the independent worker marketplace differently. They also described several cohorts: free agents were those who were making a career of independent work; casual earners were those who supplemented existing employee income with an alternative work arrangement. These two groups were independent by choice. Reluctants were those who would rather have a full-time job. Similarly, the financially strapped were those who did independent work to make ends meet. The following graphic compares the two studies.

The full-time independents or free agents in the MGI study are the high-earning cohort and are mostly specialized consultants with strong credentials and unique expertise. These represent the thousands of accomplished professionals and executives who left the traditional workplace starting in the 1980s. The exodus of many corporate women in the 1990s after the "The Mommy Track" article was greeted with concern by many corporations, yet most of these women made the choice to transform their career to something manageable on their terms. New generations of accomplished moms with impressive business credentials have followed suit. In fact, an intermediary firm called MomCorps operates franchises across the country and works specifically with this independent segment.

Similarly, exiles from high-powered consulting firms, Wall Street, and/or ad agencies recognized they could make more money with their own consulting firms, rather than as a part of a large behemoth. More importantly for some, they would also have more control over what is often a very travel-intensive life. Finally, time was a factor for many, who wanted challenging work but the ability to pursue different paths at the same time. There are consultants who are playwrights, painters, salsa dancers, or surfers. The independent lifestyle enables them fulfillment not just from work but from their muse.

The part-time segment may include some of these highly accomplished people as well, who chose to offer only a limited schedule of project work. In the recent book *Lead the Work*, the authors cite the case of TopCoder, a leading digital talent platform for expert programmers. They met several coders in a bar. They write: "The ones we met at the tavern had studied programming, but their primary employment is bartending, a job they love. Participating in Topcoder from time to time is a way to keep their hand in programming and earn a little extra cash."[14] There are also retirees who no longer want to work a full-time schedule. A somewhat-lesser-skilled area, by definition, would be those who are trying to gain new skills through consulting work. In fact, 16 percent of part-timers report they are trying to develop new competencies.

The freelance community is filled with all ages. Historically, the majority of growth in this workforce has come from workers who are 58–74. Indeed, Gen Xers and Baby Boomers in 2015 comprised the largest portions, with 33 percent and 29 percent, respectively. Seniors older than 69 represent 8 percent. The older cohorts have had the time to develop domain expertise, so it is natural that they would comprise significant portions of the professional gig working population.[15]

Millennials, those born in the 1980s and '90s, are now becoming the largest and fastest-growing segment of the Gig Economy workforce. As they enter the workforce, more and more Boomers are retiring and exiting. In the 2016 MBO partners study, Millennials made up 40 percent of the independent workforce,[16] a significant change from years past.

As the saying goes, Millennials work to live, rather than live to work. Although money is important, providing something of value and, perhaps most importantly, doing what they like is key to them. They identify with the positive side of alternative work, independence, flexibility, choice, and freedom from bureaucratic corporate environments. Many Millennials came of age during the financial crisis, when finding a traditional full-time position was difficult, so they migrated to independent work as a matter of course. They often worked as an intern or contract worker as an audition for a full-time role, so they developed an early familiarity with the notion of short-term gigs. As the economy has rebounded, many in this age group view the Gig Economy as a way to explore career alternatives. Not unsurprisingly then, 90 percent of them do not plan to stay at any one job for more than three years.[17]

Because it may take them a while to find the perfect fulfilling job, Millennials are the most adept at "side-gigging," figuring out other ways to make money aside from "regular" work. My daughter is a great example of a side-gigger. She holds a master's degree in fine arts, works for a major art auction house in New York City, and moonlights as a dog sitter through a Gig Economy digital matching firm, DogVacay, that pairs dog owners with would-be dog sitters. Though the extra money is a bonus, especially because the art world is notoriously low-paying, she is really getting a "dog fix." She loves dogs and needs to do what she loves. DogVacay helps her do that. That said, my guess is she doesn't see herself as a gig worker. She is using the digital matching platform to spend time with a dog, not to have a job. She is that occasional independent, even if she doesn't know it.

That said, Millennials do have a different view of alternative work than their older cohorts. Because they are less experienced by definition and often do not have the professional networking opportunities of more accomplished independent workers, it is harder for them to find work. They also feel more isolated as an independent than the older segments and are more concerned about the lack of benefits. Nonetheless, their desire for freedom and autonomy, suggests that this demographic group will continue to be an important part of the growth in the Gig Economy. Twenty-one percent of Millennials see independent work as a viable career path.[18]

Jody Miller, CEO of the Business Talent Group (BTG), noted this Millennial interest in the gig world first-hand. Over the last two years, she has spoken to a group of undergraduates and recent graduates at a Stanford summer business program about the independent work marketplace.

Every year, students came up to talk more about BTG and potentially see whether there might be a job at what is a very interesting firm. This year, the questions weren't about working at BTG, but rather how they could become part of the network. Moreover, these questions were coming largely from undergraduates, rather than graduates who may have some work experience. Clearly the independent life as a career is being seen as a viable option to this cohort.

A remarkable point from the 2015 MBO Partners study is that only 9 percent of the nearly 20 million full-time independents report that they are working independently by default; the corollary is over 90 percent have made independent work their career by choice, the vast majority because of the control and flexibility it affords.[19] Every time I hear someone say that the Gig Economy is not a career, I want to share this fact.

On average, these career independents have been doing this work for nearly nine years. As a result, they are very satisfied with their lifestyles. The MBO Partners study found that 80 percent of independent workers reported they were happier working on their own, and almost 75 percent of those thought the freelance lifestyle was better for their health.[20] The Conference Board puts job satisfaction of U.S. workers at 48.3 percent according to its 2015 study, so the average freelancer is much more satisfied and less worried about his/her future.[21] Further, the number of freelancers worried about their futures decreased from 40 percent in 2011 to 27 percent last year.[22] This could reflect the strengthening economy. It could also reflect increasing acceptance of the work mode. With all deference to esteemed Irish economist Charles Handy, whose quote from his most recent book opened this chapter, perhaps people are starting to notice.

Chapter 2 Key Takeaways

- The trend toward gig work has been accelerated through the elimination of the social contract between companies and employees and increased mobility of workers enhanced by technological developments.

- There are many channels through which gig workers pursue alternative work, including specialty consulting firms, staffing firms, and talent matching platforms.

- Data on the number of people working in the Gig Economy is difficult to determine, due to the lack of government data and a variety of other sources, all of which calculate the numbers slightly differently. Nonetheless, there does seem to be agreement that more than 44 million people in the United States are working in the Gig Economy.

- There is a Gig Economy pyramid, where the fewest players are making the most money providing highly specialized services at the top of the pyramid.

- All age groups participate in the Gig Economy. Millennials and Baby Boomers make up more than 70 percent of the workers.

- The Millennial cohort in the Gig Economy is growing rapidly as more millennials are drawn to the flexibility the career provides and more Boomers exit the workforce. In 2016, millennials made up 40 percent of the independent workforce.

- A solid majority, estimated at between 70 to 90 percent, of Gig Economy workers choose to work independently.

3

The Demand Side of the Gig Economy

Business is moving more quickly than ever. The advent of the Internet 25 years ago changed our regular speed to light speed. Now with social media, the primacy of mobile apps and the movement to the cloud, companies are forced to operate at warp speed or be left behind. Just consider that two of the companies that are now key engines of growth, Facebook and Twitter, are only 10 years old. The primary communication tool in many technology companies, Slack, has only been around for 3 years. The implication is that innovation is happening quickly, and by extension, adoption is occurring even faster.

> "Life moves pretty fast. If you don't stop and look around once in a while, you could miss it."
>
> —Ferris Bueller,
> *Ferris Bueller's Day Off*

If you consider language as a harbinger of fundamental societal change, then consider how different our vocabulary is from what it was 10 years ago. Words that have been added to the Oxford English dictionary in the last few years include *emoji, unfriend,* and *textspeak.* Similarly, there are the terms with new meaning. It used to be that tweeting was done by birds; now it is by the social media cognoscenti. For most Americans, the Internet and its social media offspring have been adopted faster than any other technical innovation, including radio, television, or the home computer. This adoption rate is driving the pace of business.

Five-year planning cycles are no longer valid in a world where technology can become obsolete in less than six months. As enterprise and home applications have moved to the cloud, system upgrades can occur overnight, setting a very high bar for how responsive firms need to be to the marketplace and their customers.

Similarly, as the pace of change has accelerated, customer expectations have become more demanding as well. Customers expect their systems to be online and available 24/7. As time becomes more precious, consumers want to be sure they can utilize products and services when they want them. Moreover, they also want to be able to schedule them from their mobile device, computer, or tablet, and businesses have had to adapt to deliver that functionality.

Organizations need to follow suit. Gone are the days of excruciatingly long recruiting cycles. One major Silicon Valley network company now has a mobile app for entry-level hires. It used to be when the company went to job fairs they collected resumes. Now they get them through the app, have interviews during the fairs, and extend offers the following week.

Technology companies may have the greatest bias for action in bringing in talent of all types. Other industries have not totally embraced the on-demand world, which means their business models are ripe for disruption. Healthcare, for example, is still often scheduled at the provider's convenience, rather than the consumer's. But that is changing, too. One Medical, a new player in the field backed by technology, is deviating from tradition and offering same-day appointments, online scheduling, and direct emails with doctors. Chances are, they may be setting a new normal for that industry, disrupting it with on-demand convenience.

In a recent interview with Jacob Morgan, the cofounder of the Future of Work Organization, Francine Katsoudas, the chief people officer of the global networking giant Cisco Systems, said that one of the challenges of work today is that the business moves faster than the employees.[1] Companies need to keep up; the traditional methods businesses have used to accelerate execution no longer apply, so new approaches are needed. On-demand expertise is one of them.

To thrive in the Gig Economy, it is important to understand why, when, and how businesses seek to secure high-level, on-demand expertise. Let's explore some of the key forces defining the work world today.

Why Independent Expertise Is in Demand

It's All About Projects

Twenty-five years ago, Tom Peters coined the term *projectization* in his book, *Liberation Management*. He cited my old company, M Squared, as the poster child of this trend, in which large initiatives were deconstructed into distinct tasks that could be managed as projects. Similarly, Roger Martin argued in the *Harvard Business Review* that "knowledge work never belonged in jobs in any case"; his view was that traditional jobs were designed for the industrial era and knowledge work is much better suited to projects, which is clearly illustrated by the way in which professional services firms, comprised of knowledge workers, tend to organize.[2] Major initiatives could be completed more quickly by considering which projects could be done concurrently rather than sequentially. By working concurrently, more work could be done in the same amount of elapsed time. By definition, any concurrent projects would be handled by a different team of players. Staffing these concurrent projects meant bringing in outside expertise.

Alternatively, when large initiatives are parsed into constituent parts, it can give rise to repeated serial efforts, meaning that the same person handles a certain type of specialized work on an as-needed or intermittent basis. An expert in one particular dimension of an initiative could consult to the team in that one area only, contributing episodically along the way. For a major technology player launching new platforms, for example, the customer experience expert would join the project team at a certain part of each roll-out to ascertain client sentiment. The feedback would be shared and the expert would move on.

Part of the reason for projectization is that much of the world economy is transitioning from an industrial organizational structure to a knowledge-based digital one. The hierarchies and job specialization that powered the industrial age are coexisting now with more nimble structures. The idea of performing all business activity as a series of projects completed with precise inputs of labor once seemed like an economic theory, but now as the labor markets become more efficient, the theory could become a reality. As intermediaries and digital platforms reduce the friction in the labor market, enabling efficient acquisition of just-in-time talent, we come closer to that potential. Unfortunately, many big companies are not configured to enable this throughout their organizations. Project initiatives done with resources from both within and without the organization are enabling such companies to build new muscles, muscles which, over time, will create more flexible work structures.

As multidisciplinary teams become more common place, this mode of operation becomes more powerful for companies large and small alike. Getting just the slice of talent required and, more importantly, paying only for that part that is needed, is a cost-effective way to staff a large team.

That said, as consulting firms have learned over the years, there needs to be some kind of shared experience—some kind of "glue"—for those on the team to make them come together and work cohesively. When dealing with a team comprised of employees and independent consultants who may not have a common context, this can be even more important. Whether it is a kickoff meeting to ground all team members in the rules of engagement or whether one project leader is deemed responsible for making sure all participants know how projects are handled in this particular environment, there are ways to finesse the glue. Technology provides options for virtual team cohesion as well. Many companies use collaboration tools such as Evernote and Asante to maintain a consistent communication channel for internal and external team members.

For years, M Squared worked with a major technology company doing corporate communications work. An enterprise of more than 60,000 employees worldwide had a major communications challenge to ensure everyone was on the same page about key initiatives. Because the core competency of the firm was embedded in its deep technology, it chose to bring sophisticated communications expertise into its teams on an as-needed basis. As such, we had communications consultants across many teams at the firm called on to clarify and coordinate messaging during product launches, acquisitions, or major brand events. To simplify what was a large-scale effort, we created a matrix arrangement for the client, where we provided the guidance and oversight to these communications experts who were staffed on initiative teams. We were the glue that enabled these experts to operate seamlessly within the client company whenever and wherever they were needed.

It's Just the Business Model

Advertising has historically been an industry in which freelance talent was brought in to supplement the in-house team on certain projects. Given that legacy, it is no surprise that there are any number of agencies that are building their business on the premise of a core complement of professionals bolstered by an army of freelancers. Although most of the industry does this, some tout this strategy as a key to their success. (Others are not so transparent and don't want to let their clients know how much of the work may be being done by outside resources.) The Hub in San Francisco is a case in point. According to founder D.J. O'Neill, the 15-person staff is augmented by 100 award-winning creative talents: "We don't carry the overhead of having these extremely talented creatives on our payroll—they do what they're good at, and then are gone until the next job comes along that needs their skills. We tell clients that we're able to have the output of a large agency, at a medium agency price, with small agency speed and service."[3]

Management consulting is another business that is inherently project-based and can therefore build a just-in-time staffing structure to minimize fixed costs. Highlands Consulting Group is a Sacramento-based professional services firm that provides strategic and operational consulting to its government and commercial clients. From feasibility studies to procurement to change management, its projects tend to be long-term, requiring different expertise in different phases of the engagement. The sales cycle can also be long, so maintaining a full complement of skilled consultants is an expensive proposition. It manages the cyclical nature of its business through creative use of a loyal independent network of consultants. Says CEO Mike Cappelluti:

> Since day one, we have used independent consultants to either augment our consulting capacity or provide a unique expertise. They tend to have at least 10 years of consulting experience. Many like to take time off between projects or want to work part-time. We integrate them into project teams so well that clients can't distinguish between our employees and our contractors—we are one seamless, integrated, high-performing team. We only contract with consultants who share our values of client service, integrity, being a team player, learning, and truly enjoy our chosen profession. And we love it when our independent contractors tell us we are their number one firm to work with. They stick with

us long term, which save us time and money in vetting qualified resources.[4]

Another interesting example of this deliberate strategic approach is A Connect, a global consulting firm that created highly specialized project teams for its clients by relying upon its own independent professional network of very senior subject matter experts. Their tag line even touts this strategy: "Human Resourcefulness—Globally Delivered."[5] Independent Professionals (IPs) in the A Connect world are carefully screened by the firm. Once assigned to a project, they are given A Connect cards and an A Connect email address. When the project is ended, the IP moves on, although a business relationship remains; in between assignments, the IP is free to use office space at an A Connect office.

Insourcing Expertise

Another dimension of business moving so fast is that often as new opportunities arise, a company does not have the expertise to evaluate them in a timely and comprehensive way. To be able to move quickly, the company needs to bring that non-resident expertise in-house. For example, the decision to move to another geography, especially an international one, can be a difficult one if no one within the enterprise has first-hand knowledge of the new market. Similarly, a product line expansion could bring with it new suppliers, distribution channels, or customers. Insider knowledge of any of those new dimensions could be of great value.

As such, many companies turn to the independent consulting marketplace to bring that precise expertise in house for these new ventures. The Business Talent Group (BTG) is a specialty consulting firm that provides a vetted network of senior-level independent consulting talent who work on projects that average $100,000 in fees. Many of the free agent consultants are alumni from large brand-name consulting firms, so they offer an alternative to high-priced solutions consultants, such as McKinsey and Bain, at a lower price point. Similarly, M Squared Consulting hires its own senior consulting engagement managers and uses independent consultants from its network to fill out its project team.

These projects can have major strategic import for clients. Some of BTG's recent projects include helping a bio pharma firm launch a new drug when it did not have the internal expertise, developing a global retail strategy for a major player that was expanding to Europe and covering the maternity leave of a senior manager in a financial services company whose responsibility including leading a major new product launch.[6]

On a smaller scale, many firms may want an expert opinion about some key topic. A private equity firm, for example, may want an opinion about the future of LED lighting before considering the purchase of an LED manufacturing facility. Zintro provides just that. Founder Stewart Lewtan, following the sale of his software company, did some "spot" consulting with the Gerson Lehrman Group (GLG), a firm known to provide expert advice in phone calls or short consulting projects to private equity firms or in expert witness roles. Lewtan was surprised at how high a price GLG was able to command even though the experts were only receiving a fraction of that fee. He surmised that a significant portion of that cost came from the highly manual back-end process GLG used at the time to do its matching. He brought his technology skills to bear to address that inefficiency and created a platform with proprietary algorithms that enabled him to more efficiently match projects with experts. Many other sites, including other expert networks, now use that technology to help identify experts for clients. Zintro's network is a mix of consultants, scientists, and engineers, who tend to be specialists in a very precise and sometimes arcane segment of their industries. Zintro also realized that certain companies—market research firms, for example—need to ask many short but complex questions, so it developed subscription-fee models for those clients.

Companies need to bring in precision expertise in varying amounts to compete in today's marketplace. If BTG provides the right slice of talent for large-scale projects, Zintro can measure out just one teaspoon for those in need of an answer or opinion before making a critical decision.

Buy What You Need

As the saying goes, "Why buy a pig if all you want is some sausage?" Many companies do not need to invest in a regular hire for either finite efforts or seasonal ones. A recent *Forbes* article focused on a growing San Francisco retailer of educational products for children, Little Passports. A $30 million and growing operation now, it had to tap the angel investor market when venture capitalists did not buy into its educational subscription product idea. Instead of doing the all-out media blitz that generous funding would have enabled, Little Passports hired a freelancer marketer to help grow the business.[7] Many similarly bootstrapped enterprises tap the independent work marketplace to get just the expertise they need and can afford.

Buying just what you need in the independent expertise marketplace is also a practice of the Alliance of CEOs. The Alliance of Chief Executives is an organization that brings leaders throughout Northern California together to enable CEOs and C-level executives to exchange strategic insights, refine their leadership skills, and make valuable connections. I am one of 20 directors at the Alliance. Each of us facilitates a private, monthly meeting with 10–12 CEOs, designed for them to explore strategic business issues with other leaders and to gather confidential input around these issues and opportunities. The directors are all accomplished businesspeople. Many, as I am, are former CEOs; others combine a wealth of business experience with consulting, teaching, or investing. Regardless of our backgrounds, we are all consultants to the Alliance. The Alliance could have hired an employee (or two) to manage all its CEO groups, as each group meets only once a month. Instead, the Alliance opted to contract with a diverse group of senior executives who bring a similarly diverse array of experiences to the role. In so doing, the Alliance is able to tap the insights and expertise of a cohort of accomplished individuals, thereby providing a far more robust service delivery model for its members.

Fresh Eyes

Many firms turn to consulting firms to get a fresh perspective on a problem to turn up what could be a new solution. In his book *A More Beautiful Question*, Warren Berger describes the problem of internal experts. They don't have to ask questions because they just *know*. Outsiders, on the other hand, can come into an environment and be much more able to ask creative "why" and "what if" questions, because they are not shackled by what they know. Independent expertise can provide that same type of outside view that can lead to innovative results.

A recent *Wall Street Journal* article pointed out that many CFOs, faced with activist investors and roiled markets, are turning to consultants to help them grapple with an increasingly complex world. As one researcher noted, "Consultants are like plumbers; they're hired when there's something wrong with your heating system and it's not economically worth you training to be a plumber."[8]

Sometimes fresh eyes are needed because the internal team has worked an issue for so long, they can no longer discern the nuances of the problem. In his recent book, *Smarter Faster Better,* Charles Duhig talked about the problems experienced by the FBI in building an integrated system to capture all sorts of criminal activities with the hope that sophisticated big data searches would find patterns and yield clues to ongoing investigations. Years of effort across multiple projects and more than $170 million dollars were spent on the system, but it was so unreliable that agents still used file cards to collect data. It took a Wall Street–trained systems developer who approached the issue with a different lens and new strategies like agile programming to turn the project around.

Similarly, an outsider can be best when internal politics make an issue too hot to handle. In some companies, difficult issues are ignored, because no one wants to open Pandora's box. An unbiased observer is often then best person to open that box. A consultant can be seen as non-aligned and therefore more objective in his or her viewpoint.

If no one is willing to take drastic action to address a problem, it may require an outside point of view. M Squared was asked to intervene in the case of an international microfiber producer with a poorly performing division. The CEO, management, and the board were at odds about the path forward. Tensions were high about which course would be pursued, so an external expert was sought to evaluate the options. The consultant was able to effectively assess that the returns of this division could not become sufficiently robust to yield the type of pre-tax returns enjoyed by the other business units and expected by the shareholders. On the other hand, he was able to objectively evaluate the underlying technology and found that it was highly marketable in a host of different types of applications. He recommended the sale of the division to a company in another industry who could utilize the technology in a very different and profitable way. That latter perspective is one that almost certainly would not have emerged from an internal resource, and it was that strategy that offered the best business and financial solution.

Finally, sometimes the inner circle is not willing to tell the CEO that a direction could be ill-advised. Good consultants can make these calls. They know that although they are beholden to their clients, they are also tied to the business success of their client as well. Sometimes referred to as the "Emperor's New Clothes" problem, consultants are paid to deliver what might not be good news to the CEO.

Organizational Holes

As Woody Allen said, 90 percent of success is showing up. When someone doesn't show up in a leadership team, that can be a problem. However, things happen. The unexpected departure of a key manager may require an interim solution. Similarly, a sudden illness or a medical leave may also need coverage. Much as companies have long looked to temporary staff to help out for administrative staff and support team members to ensure no lost productivity during a vacancy, they now know they can handle a management vacancy in the same fashion.

For many years, we offered a maternity leave coverage product for our clients. We covered the maternity leave of HR managers, CFOs, executive directors, and marketing group managers, to name just a few. We worked with the clients before the fact to determine how the company envisioned handling the job during the maternity leave. In some cases, responsibilities could be doled out to others on the team, so that the role that needed to be filled was not a full-time equivalent (FTE). In other cases, the leave presented an opportunity to provide more responsibility to a subordinate. In some of these situations, our project was to backfill the subordinate, rather than the manager on leave.

Many industries today are facing an increasing vacancy problem with the retirement of the Baby Boomers. Certain defense contractors have mandatory retirement at age 65. Unfortunately, the new hire that will take the place of the retiree does not have near the experience of his or her predecessor. Certain specialty staffing firms immediately recruit the retirees into a network of independent workers with the skill sets and security clearances needed by these defense contractors. In some cases, they sell the retiree back to the firm. The 65-year-old may not be able to be an employee any longer, but he or she can be a consultant. (Curious, I know.)

The acquisition environment is another key area for interim talent. The acquirer often needs to better understand what skills are resident in the acquired team and may be reluctant to hire full-time employees until the new capabilities are better understood. In the meantime, work needs to be done, so interim hires present a great solution. This can be especially true when there are many departures in the acquired firm in which managers may want to take control of their own career destiny. As such, keeping things going during a transition may require some additional expertise.

We worked on one project in which a large pharmaceutical company was buying a growing biotech business. The pharmaceutical and biotech worlds have some similarities, but in many ways they are dramatically different. One of the key differences is compensation. The HR director at the pharma company knew that she was not an expert in the prevailing practices in bio technology. The biotech firm had a very junior human resource staff and not the level of expertise needed to facilitate a smooth integration of the new team. We provided a senior-level HR expert with deep expertise in the biotech world to assist the acquisition team in developing new compensation and retention programs.

Teamwork

Many firms use just-in-time talent as a step in their hiring process. The "try before you buy" model is well established. For many companies, bringing someone in on a project basis is a real-time way to evaluate their fit in the organization. For startups, this is a very powerful tool. "For a startup, a bad hire can be devastating, so the Gig Economy is our go-to strategy for finding the best people," says Peter Sobotta, cofounder and CEO of @returnlogic. "The most successful way to court talent is to offer small, contracted projects that deliver an immediate ROI to the company and determine if the individual is a good recruit."[9]

At M Squared, we knew certain key roles were mission critical to our success. As such, we regularly staffed a "bench" to ensure we never had vacancies in our key client-facing areas. Key among these were our client service managers (CSM), the people who would actually match consultants to projects. We identified skilled consultants in recruiting and executive search. At our expense, we would train them in our platform and practices, and then we would say goodbye, with the understanding that we might call them at any time to pinch hit for us as part of our team. When business volume spiked and we did not have internal capacity or if we knew we might have extended vacations or maternity leaves, we could call on this bench to cover the gap. Our bench was always larger than our needs, because we knew these good consultants had clients of their own and might be too busy when we made our call. For a time-sensitive business like ours, this was a tremendous tool.

It turned out to be a recruiting tool as well. When the time came for us to hire a new manager into that group, we looked to one of our bench players who had been a VP of HR. Not only did she become part of that team, but ultimately, when we hired our own VP of HR, she got the job. She knew, as much as anyone, how strategically we used talent to empower our team.

The Need for Speed

And of course, the urgency for output today drives many to secure whatever extra expertise they can to launch new initiatives, match seasonal capacity surges, or handle non-core tasks that just need to get done.

For example, just recently Lesley Berglund, the CEO of the WISE Academy, a growing Napa Valley company that provides leadership development and sales training programs for the wine industry, contacted me because she wanted advice on how she could secure specialized expertise to design a new curriculum for the courses she provides to wineries. She has an exciting new launch of content through a joint venture with a major business school and wants to get these new executive education programs in production as soon as possible. Given their international growth as well as the demands of current clients, current staff would be hard-pressed to build out this whole new curriculum element quickly. An experienced instructional designer will enable this exciting new program to launch quickly.

This story is being repeated in startups around the country. Another colleague of mine, Ranjan Sinha, started Heart'n Spice, a personalized nutrition meal-delivery service that works with major hospitals and weight loss programs to provide healthy, fresh meal options for members. The 18-month-old company needed to grow quickly, so Ranjan, a serial entrepreneur well acquainted with effective ways to get things done, reached out for web developers and other technical resources through various digital talent marketplaces to accelerate the development of the service.

Light Polymers is a Bay Area startup in the materials chemistry industry, which is dominated by large international chemical companies, such as Dow, Dupont, and BASF. It uses independent expertise of many sorts, from retired executives who can help them ramp up in Asia, to graphic artists secured from digital platforms, to post doc students in R&D. CEO Marc McConnaughey says, "We are gigging almost everything at Light Polymers to break through and go faster, be more flexible, deliver in one day rather than 3 months and just be totally different than the industry in which we work."[10]

The message is simple: any firm not reaching out to try to leverage its internal team with external expertise may be losing ground on the competition.

Implications for New Economy Workers

Given these workplace trends, how do those workers in the On-Demand Economy optimize for success?

Clearly urgency is a critical success factor. Companies want to respond quickly and need access to the right resources as efficiently as possible. Being in the right places for clients to find you when they have the urgent need is key to the success of today's consultants. Those "right places" will depend on your specialty, but they include being in someone's contact base, professional association, and LinkedIn group. (We will talk about these strategies more in Chapter 6.)

Moreover, companies need to be sure that these external resources can be brought into their organizations quickly, and that the assimilation process of getting the resources up and running is timely and seamless. Your ability to adapt to new organizations and quickly come up to speed is critical.

Insourced resources need to be ready to hit the ground running, so any frictions that could slow the pace need to be identified and reduced. Enablers to an assignment, such as contracts or an insurance certification, need to be in place. (We will cover those logistical issues more in Chapter 8.)

Also, given the pace of business, a good consultant needs to check in regularly with his or her client to ensure the project is on track, because waiting until it is completed only to find it wasn't what the client expected doesn't make for a successful engagement. This recalibration needs to be a regular part of a consultant's business process.

For companies trying to operate quickly, building a bench can be a powerful tool. It takes the question of "Where will I find someone to do this for me tomorrow?" off the table. Also, the knowledge transfer after the project is concluded is a key issue that many companies often do not consider. It is one thing to get a project completed, but if the best expertise on the subject leaves your organization as a result, the firm hasn't expanded its intellectual capital. Consultants should recognize this need from the get-go and design that knowledge-sharing step into all projects. These elements form the business model that will enable a company and consultant to thrive in this new world of work. In the chapters to come, we will explore ways for you to ensure your company and its services meld with that business model.

Chapter 3 Key Takeaways

- The rapid evolution of technology has shortened the business cycle and left companies resource challenged to meet the demands of the marketplace.

- Companies use on-demand expertise for many reasons, chief among them:

  - Exploiting projectization.

  - Insourcing expertise.

  - Gaining an external perspective.

  - Buying only what you need.

  - Filling organizational holes.

  - Testing future hires.

  - Ensuring fast turnaround.

- Gig workers need to meet the urgency need of companies to make it in the new world of work and provide deliberate approaches to ensure the client gets the desired end result.

- Companies should consider building a bench of on-demand expertise to manage capacity in a time-sensitive business.

4

Building Your Independent Brand

At about the time my first book came out, there was a lot of attention on personal branding. My book *A New Brand of Expertise,* Dan Pink's *Free Agent Nation,* and Peter Montoya's *The Brand Called You* were all in the marketplace offering assistance to those who were launching their future endeavors by creating a personal brand. And that advice has just kept coming, with recent offerings such as *The Freelancer's Bible.* As such, is there really anything more to say?

> "Your brand is what people say about you when you are not in the room."
>
> —Jeff Bezos

How can there not be, given the digital world in which we live? Back in the day, the process was about assembling your body of work, identifying your value proposition, and staking out your space. That remains true today, but now all of those efforts also involve your digital history. It is said that even a child of age 2 has a digital footprint. Fortunes have been made erasing digital footprints by the likes of Reputation.com and their personal solutions product, Reputation Defender. When I taught HR to college seniors we regularly discussed this issue, and many didn't recognize that the bawdy photo of the beer bash and red Solo cups that was posted on Facebook back in their college days can live on in infamy.

But even if you have no digital mistakes, you do have a digital voice. And in the world today, that voice is a very important component of the consultant's brand. Ten years ago, a potential employer would look at your resume. Now a client will Google you and check out your LinkedIn profile before ever considering you for a role. By the way, it may not be your credentials that catch their eye, but rather the typo in your bio. Let's face it: Some people take less care with their LinkedIn profiles than they do with their resumes, and that can lead to a less-than-stellar impression. But let's start with the basics, and then advance to digital branding and how your social media efforts can support your practice.

First Things First

If you are already consulting or have already made the decision to do so, skip to the next section of this chapter. For those in the consideration stage, read on. As I discussed at length in my first book, *A New Brand of Expertise*,[1] there are risks inherent in starting a consulting practice. As such, there are three key questions that you must ponder before you proceed.

First, do you really have expertise someone would buy? No one wants a mediocre expert. If your skills aren't strong enough to claim mastery, then think no further about it. That said, different fields have different thresholds and experiential domains. It is unlikely that a recent college graduate would have significant expertise in building a project management office for a multinational corporation. However, that same individual may have deep knowledge of digital media strategies for small companies. So when assessing your expertise quotient, be sure to keep it in the context of the types of assignments you could procure from a particular segment of companies.

Assuming your skills are marketable, there are two corollary questions: **how much do you need to make annually,** and **is there enough of a market for your expertise to support your lifestyle?** The annual earnings you require from consulting is a personal question. It is contingent on your savings, income from other sources, and your spending patterns. If you are the sole provider and have regular monthly expenses, launching what could be a career with an uncertain income stream can be daunting. You need to budget carefully and make some critical assumptions about the income levels you could achieve, the time it will take for you to secure those engagements, and the downtime between assignments. Ironically, the new digital platform world can provide a cushion for such a dramatic step; as you launch your consulting practice, you can also drive for Uber on the side or do weekly TaskRabbit gigs to generate income during the slow periods. This ability to be able to depend on side gigs through digital platforms may be contributing to the growth of the professional independent work trend.

Alternatively, many consultants are senior managers or entrepreneurs who have opted to leave their corporate or operating roles. For them, consulting is not so much of an income imperative as it is a way to remain intellectually engaged. The recent McKinsey Global Institute study would refer to them as "casual independent workers." Many Boomer retirees also fit into this category. After early retirement from a corporation, they still want to work, but on their own terms. Potential for sufficient income for this group is not a major factor.

For those who need to assess the income factor, the market demand question may be harder to assess before the fact. You may not know until you are out there selling what the reception is on the part of the buyer. One option is to set a time line (i.e., I will give this a shot for three months or six months to see if I can get traction). If you do such a pilot, try to make it as true to life as possible to make the outcome as meaningful as possible. Similarly, another option is to ask trusted colleagues in organizations to help you understand the market by telling you what they might pay for the types of services you could offer.

Digital talent sites such as Hourly Nerd or Zintro can offer some ideas about the going rate for projects, but the bid and offer structure could understate fees; consultants in need of work may underbid to secure attention from cost sensitive buyers. For those in technical disciplines, gigs on Fiverr or Upwork can be artificially low, because any of the contractors listed in these sites are from low-wage geographies; it can be hard to be a low-priced bidder when competing with gig workers in Pakistan or Bulgaria. (Indeed, the programmers I secured on Fiverr for my book website were from Romania, Morocco, and the UK.)

Specialty consulting firms such as M Squared or the Business Talent Group (BTG) may be the best source for information about market rates for your skills. Keep in mind, though, these firms are not in the business of career counseling for new consultants; however, they are always looking for qualified talent. You should be able to tell from their onboarding process how interesting and therefore saleable your background is to them.

And one last note: If you get excited when reviewing the digital talent platform sites, because many of the gigs look like something right up your alley, keep in mind that many of these sites have many shoppers but far fewer buyers. In fact, some sites even rate the buyers to indicate that have actually hired people when they posted projects.

You Are an Island

John Donne said, "No man is an island," but he did not know about the independent worker modus operandi. As an independent consultant, you are an island because you are totally on your own.

You must be able to look to yourself for direction, motivation, reinforcement, and consolation. Professional associations and colleagues can provide some support, but for the most part, it is up to you to create a fulfilling work environment. In many cases, you will be working off site and not in the client environment, which can add to the isolation. For some, working at the client site can be just as isolating, because you may be seen as an outsider.

Some consultants partner with other independents to get more of a sense of community. Others rent offices at coworking facilities like WeWork, as doing so provides community as well as office space, administrative support, and technology assistance. However, these services come at a cost. In San Francisco, the cheapest WeWork plan is $400/month. If your primary motive in securing space is for social connection rather than efficiency, you may want to rethink your plan.

Think back on your career to any telecommuting experiences or home office work. Were your productive or distracted? Were you rejuvenated when you reconnected with your colleagues, or did you wish you were able to work from home more often? Did you find the need to meet up with people for lunch or coffee to balance your day? If, on reflection, you prefer a vibrant office environment, you may want to proceed slowly, because the energy you get from others may be tough to replace in the independent consulting environment.

Can You Say *No?*

In the management novella *The Five Temptations of a CEO*, Patrick Lencioni posits that one common flaw of a CEO is the inability to deliver bad news. To avoid confrontation, he or she relies on metrics to make poor performance clear, rather than calling it out directly. Because anyone who is setting up a consulting practice is the CEO of his or her own firm, this flaw could be fatal, because you need to be able to say no to a client for many reasons.

First, you need to be able to tell a client that they are wrong. They may not like that answer, but you need to give it. The consultant who tells a client what they want to hear, rather than bad news, will hurt his or her practice in the long run. Remember: you are being paid for your expertise, not your political skills.

Second, you may need to tell a client that something they may ask you to do is not within the scope of a project. As employees, we are all used to doing whatever the boss says; if you are working on X and are asked to do Y, you pivot and do so. As a consultant, it is not that simple. You contract for deliverables. If the client asks for something above and beyond those deliverables, you are facing scope creep, and the contract must be renegotiated. That is a difficult conversation to have with a client, but it is an essential one.

Finally, if the client asks you to do work that is outside of your skill set, you need to say no to that as well. Often a consultant will deliver a recommendation, and the client will then ask the consultant to implement it. The consultant may be appropriate for that role—or may not be. It is better to decline the follow-on work that is not in your sweet spot, than to take it on and perform poorly. This is emblematic of a true consultant: a person who is highly ethical and fully client-focused, so much so, that he or she is willing to turn down work to best serve the client.

An organizational consultant once did a major restructure for a large corporate client. The client then asked her to manage the recruiting process for the new senior-management role envisioned in the new corporate structure. She agreed, despite the fact that she had no expertise in executive search or recruiting. She had the hubris of many a successful consultant; *How hard can it be?* she thought. Luckily before she lost all the goodwill earned from her brilliant organizational design, she came to us for advice. We were able to intervene and bring in a search expert to find the new hire. The original consultant became part of the interview process, which was an appropriate role for her. Being able to say no and knowing when to say no are key elements to ensure the quality of your engagement outcomes.

Your Brand Basics

For those that have decided to become an independent consultant as well as for those who are already in business, let's discuss some key elements of personal branding.

Classic studies of consumer goods branding show that the highest returns come to the brands with the highest level of recognition and brand equity. By extension, the greatest returns to your investors—*aka* you—will accrue as you strengthen your brand.

As it does with any business, the branding discussion comes down to your core values. Simply put, your brand is what you stand for and what you deliver to your clients. What value proposition do you offer? What are the tangible and intangible attributes that a buyer will assign to the services you deliver? And how will your clients interact with your brand? Based on that interaction, what is your brand personality?

I know for some this may seem a bit touchy-feely, so let's put it in tangible terms. Think about your consulting practice in terms of the approach you take, the way your work, and your outcomes. In terms of approach, is what you bring to the table your ability to come up with a creative solution, or your knack of digging in to a problem? Do you bill yourself as an expert, a mentor, or a coach? Similarly, is your work mode one where you pitch in to do whatever the team needs or one where you go off and do research and come back with an answer? Finally, what is the nature of your end result? Is the client buying a consensus solution, a wild new design, or a 30-page white paper?

The following table gives you some descriptions of various approaches, work modes, and outcomes. Think about the ones that most apply to your business as well as others that come to mind. Which of these attributes would be core to you and the work you want to do? This might help you isolate the set of core values for your business.

Values Table		
Approach	**Work Mode**	**Outcomes**
Collaborative	Process-Oriented	Consensus-Based
Data-Driven	Energizing	Provocative
Analytical	Interactive	Reasoned
Creative	Research Intensive	Innovative
Patented	Comprehensive	Actionable
Unique	Technology-Enabled	Fit Culturally
Expert-Based	Team-Oriented	Far-Reaching
Advisory	Independent	High Impact
Mentor-Like	Versatile	Report-Based
Intuitive	Thoughtful	Quotable
Time-Tested		Expandable

A Consulting SWOT

Another way to think about your brand is to approach the question as a strategy consultant would. A key aspect of any business strategy is a SWOT, a strategy consulting acronym for evaluating strengths, weaknesses, opportunities, and threats.

In the strengths and weaknesses section, you are defining where you do and do not play in your functional expertise area. For example, a CFO may recognize her expertise is in financially distressed companies, rather than stable or growing ones. A marketing communications consultant may be expert at employee communications but not so experienced at investor relations. You need to be brutally honest with yourself to critique what you do and don't do well. Given that we don't always see ourselves as others see us, reaching out to coworkers, bosses, and subordinates to get a sense of how they see you can be well worth the effort.

To the extent that it plays into your consulting practice, include soft skills as well, such as leadership, management style, and communication skills. Client management, team-building, and other soft skills can play a crucial role in the management of your engagements, and as such have marketability in the independent consulting marketplace.

Personal Brand SWOT Analysis

STRENGTHS

- Key skills, both hard and soft
- Achievements
- Results

WEAKNESSES

- Functional gaps
- Dislikes
- Failures

OPPORTUNITIES

Related Industries   New Technologies   Transferable Skills

THREATS

- Other competitors
- Economic conditions
- Pricing

Similarly, recognize the voids in your background. If you have only worked in one company for 10 years (so have limited exposure to different approaches) or if you never managed more than a small team, recognize those weaknesses. A CFO looking for interim CFO gigs in the startup world, for example, needs to understand that the lack of pre-IPO experience could be a weakness in that space.

Your weaknesses are not just the areas where you have limited experience, they are also the things you do not like to do. It is a truism of human nature that you do best what you love. As such, recognize those things that don't float your boat. If you have done enough Excel modeling to last you the rest of your life, recognize that fact. Your weakness is not that you are not good at modeling; rather it is something you choose not to do.

If you have had a significant business failure, this could be a weakness or a strength. A sales manager who never got a team productive might be a great salesperson, rather than a great manager. Alternatively, a product manager who launched a product that failed may have learned a tremendous amount about what not to do in a consumer product launch. Again, the more honest you can be about your own limitations, the more authentic the outcome of your SWOT will be.

Opportunities represent transferable skills that may play in new markets or industries. If you are early in a particular technology, your ability to bring that knowledge to other industries that have not yet adopted the new technology could be a powerful asset. Digital marketing, for example, is now a highly valued skill set, especially in old-line businesses that may have been slow to embrace social media.

Again, one thing to consider in conducting your SWOT is getting input from past managers, coworkers, and subordinates; 360-degree feedback is a great tool for the evaluation of performance in organizations. It can also inform your analysis. In my years in YPO (the Young President's Organization), we have done these types of personal assessments regularly. The key is to have a short set of questions which enables commentary. Travis Kalanick, the CEO of Uber, use a simple but disciplined feedback system called T3B3, which stands for top three skills and bottom three skills,[2] an approach which could be easily adapted. Just let your associates know you are not looking for compliments, but rather looking to identify the "secret sauce" that you bring to the table. You may be surprised at the things you learn.

Positioning Your Practice

Once you have completed this exercise, you are ready to create and position your brand. First define the value proposition you will deliver to your target market. What will be your niche? How will you differentiate yourself from other service providers? Why should clients buy from you? The value proposition is like a cornerstone, so take care to define it wisely.

It may end up being your catch phrase on Twitter and LinkedIn. If it is not worthy of serving that function, you may not have identified the right value proposition.

I recently heard Curt Carlson, former CEO of the Stanford Research Institute (SRI), speak on the subject of value propositions. He observed that most companies do not define the elements of a value proposition. He offered a four-pronged approach for companies that can be applicable for independent professionals as well. His acronym for the parts of a value proposition are NABC,[3] in which:

- **N** is the description of the need being addressed.
- **A** is the approach to address the need.
- **B** is the benefit net of costs for successfully meeting the need.
- **C** is the competition for meeting the need that exists in the marketplace.

Thinking of your practice in these terms can help you refine your value proposition, which help you position yourself in the marketplace.

Positioning can be helpful in developing that thought leadership niche and is often overlooked in a service business. In the early days of M Squared, one of our branding consultants worked with us in the development of our new payroll service, Collabrus. They put us through a great exercise during which we had to create a very precise statement. Interestingly, it addresses the very NABC elements espoused by Carlson.

POSITIONING STATEMENT

For _____ (1)
who _____ (2),
my brand/company is
a_____ (3)
that _____ (4).
My brand is different from other
_____ (5)
because _____ (6)

Where the blanks can be filled in as follows:
1. **Target audience**
2. **Client perception**
3. **Generic description**
4. **Key benefit**
5. **Competitive products**
6. **Reasons why/value proposition**

We came up with this:

For companies who use independent talent and are concerned about independent contractor compliance, Collabrus is a risk management solution that eliminates the risk and penalties of employee misclassification. It is different from other payroll companies because it specializes in independent consultant contractors, offering a suite of services tailored to their needs.

A marketing consultant may come up with this:

For companies who need to jump-start their digital marketing efforts and feel unsure how to proceed, The Digital Whisperer is a full service digital marketing firm that creates digital marketing strategies that deliver metrics and results. The Digital Whisperer is different from other social media consulting firms, because it tailors the digital spend to your specific brand.

Critical in this example is the answer provided in blank number 5, the competing products. In this example, the competition could have been an in-house department or an advertising agency. In fact, there can be a number of competitors for a service, so one way to do this exercise is to make the statement for every type of competitor. This is a good exercise because it makes you define your core offering, isolate your target customers, identify your competition, and differentiate yourself in the market.

A good additional step is to specify not only the ideal assignments for your brand, but also to consider the assignments you would not assume. One of the benefits of working for yourself is the ability to pick and choose your work environments, industries, and locations. If you would never want to work for a tobacco company, for example, own that. If you want to limit your travel for family reasons, make sure it is clear that the brand called you is in control of your travel schedule.

We once had an interim treasurer assignment for a major not-for-profit heathcare system. The consultant who performed the three-month role loved the compassionate mission of the organization, and, similarly, the healthcare system was thrilled with her contribution. The client ultimately asked to make her an offer to be the "permanent" treasurer. Our consultant considered this long and hard. Although she loved the short-term assignment, the healthcare system had ties to the Catholic Church, and our consultant did not agree with the Church view on homosexuality. The short-term engagement was fine, but a longer-term role was not consistent with her core values; it did not fit her brand.

Another way to expand your personal brand concept is to think of a narrative. In their branding book, *Getting to Like: How to Boost Your Personal and Professional Brand to Expand Opportunities, Grow your Business and Achieve Financial Success*, authors Jeremy Goldman and Ali Zagot extol the virtues of building a brand narrative. They suggest developing a narrative around the mnemonic RAPTURE.[4]

- **R**elevant: The story of your brand should have key core elements.

- **A**uthentic: Your narrative must be true and moving.

- **P**ersuasive: It must convince people to discover more about you.

- **T**imely: It must be up to date and play to today's world and issues.

- **U**nderstandable: It must be easy to understand.

- **R**elatable: People must be able to imagine what it is like to be in your shoes and why those shoes matter.

- **E**ducational: It should be your elevator pitch and educate audiences about who you really are.

The authors go on to suggest that the "rapture methodology" is especially useful for those who may be changing careers or launching new initiatives. The narrative about how you came to do this, why you are the right person to handle a certain type of problem, and why clients should consider you above all others is critical to your success.

Just to be clear, I see these approaches not as something that needs to go on your website, but rather as a great organizing construct for you to gain clarity in your messaging. Perhaps the most important result will be focusing on the area in which true subject matter expertise can be cultivated. You want to be a thought leader in your space, since that will earn client respect.

From the value proposition, you can set a brand image. The brand image is the look and feel of what you project to your target clients. It starts with your practice name and extends through to logos, tag lines, websites, and any other marketing materials. It is your packaging as you productize your services.

An event planner in the corporate meeting space, for example, would have a very different image than one planning not-for-profit galas. The former may want to project values of corporate formality, technological competence, and professionalism, whereas the latter may want to evoke social responsibility, creative execution, and cost consciousness.

The brand image creates an advantage for your practices because it reinforces your message. In the prior example, a firm called the Corporate Meetings Group would already be positioned appropriately with CFO clients. Imagery would be formal and elegant in colors that were rich and luxurious. Whereas an event company called the Fun Comes, would go with whimsical images and wild colors to demonstrate its creative bent.

Consultants interested in getting a totally new take on their brand image may want to check out 99Designs.com. This is a crowd-sourced design platform with more than 1.3 million freelance designers. You provide information about your business and indicate what you want (a logo, a brand identity package, a website design, etc.). 99Designs launches a contest on the platform where designers compete to win your business. They come up with ideas, and you choose the one you like.

Communicating Your Brand in the Digital World

It used to be that your resume along with a brochure was the primary way you communicated your brand. Now in the digital world, there are a host of additional options. Regardless of the marketing channel, several key rules apply:

- Do not lie. According to a Career Builder survey, 58 percent of candidates for full time employment lied on their resume.[5] It could be that consultants are more honest. You need to be accurate and transparent.

- Similarly, do not exaggerate responsibilities. Fifty-four percent of candidates in that same study embellished their backgrounds to their detriment.[6]

- Lead with your accomplishments, not your job titles. Clients buy expertise, insight, and the comfort that the project will be handled correctly. Emphasize those aspects of your background. Moreover, titles mean different things in different enterprises. A public relations specialist role at Apple would be very different from one at the professional services firm Young and Rubicam.

- Don't include early career experiences that are no longer relevant to your expertise. If you want to be complete, say something like "Spent five years pursuing a career in real estate before transitioning to technology."

- Highlight your thought leadership. If you don't already have the content that demonstrates your thought leadership, begin to develop it in the social media space.

- Make sure any text is perfect. There should be no typos, correct punctuation, perfect grammar, and formatting consistency.

So now that we have those basic ground rules, let's discuss your overall brand communication strategy. In today's world, any consultant, regardless of specialty, needs a solid resume as well as a dynamic LinkedIn profile. The following section will offer tips on how to optimize your LinkedIn profile.

In certain specialties, such as digital marketing, a personal website is a virtual requirement, because it is an extension of your brand. Seeing how you set up the site, its navigation, its SEO optimization, the RSS feeds, and other links you may deploy, says something about your expertise in the field. A site like that would not showcase the skills of a financial expert specializing in bankruptcy. That bankruptcy expert, though, may want to write thought leadership pieces for journals, blogs, or LinkedIn to demonstrate his or her knowledge of a highly complex issue.

Those in communications or journalism may want to have a regular blog, which could be part of a website or separate blog site. Your site should be linked to content aggregators like Tumblr to increase your reach. The blog is a brand extension because it demonstrates your skill at writing.

Similarly, blogs and/or regular content posts are also good tools for those who want to demonstrate thought leadership on a topic. In my case, I blog about the Gig Economy on my website (marionmcgovern.com). I post the link to LinkedIn, Tumblr, Twitter, and sometimes Quora. I will manually port that content to certain digital platforms that do not have natural linkages, such as ExecRank, where the interface is not established. These steps add to the overhead of developing content to share, but they extend the reach of the message.

Speaking engagements can be a big brand boost, as they provide a real-time audience that can be extended in the digital world. In considering speaking gigs, whether a TED talk or a talk to a Rotary club, be sure to see if there will be a video of your remarks, because these can be featured on your personal website or in social media postings. Similarly, provide your audience with a custom hashtag and encourage real-time tweeting of your content to further build your social media brand.

Twitter can also enhance your business branding. Tweets that reinforce your area of expertise are always good, but most users tweet about business, sports, events, and random observations. As such, Twitter can bring out the authenticity of someone; she may be a great cyber consultant, but she is also a Giants fan, based on her Twitter feed. Interesting.

Other social media channels depend on your expertise domain. Pinterest may be important for someone in food, art, or apparel. A YouTube channel could be a differentiator for those with a library of video content, such as trainers or keynote speakers. Photo sites such as Instagram could be valuable for image intensive businesses like photography, art, or design.

Facebook is a wild card. Some people, including me, use it personally but not for business; I don't "friend" my business colleagues unless they are friends. Similarly, I would link to my students on LinkedIn, but not friend them on Facebook. That said, one of my MBA students worked in trucking. He maintained that Facebook was critical to his customer relationship management practices with his heavy construction clients in the Northwest. They were not on LinkedIn, but they were all over Facebook. If you choose to use Facebook, you may want to consider setting up a business page for your practice, to separate it from your personal page.

Additionally, consultants that may be in B2C, versus B2B, may need a Facebook business presence for their practice. For example, a wedding planner may need a Facebook following more than a corporate events planner.

One thing to remember about all of these vehicles, whether websites or social media sites, is the additional time needed to maintain them. A blog has no value if you don't blog regularly. LinkedIn and Twitter require a modicum of curation to make any kind of brand impact. The wonderful line from *Field of Dreams*, "If you build it, they will come," is not true in the digital world. And finally, blogs and websites cost money in terms of development costs, and maintenance and hosting fees.

The basic questions as you define your brand communication strategy are these:

- What channels and/or vehicles will demonstrate my skills to my potential buyers?
- Where are my potential buyers most likely to see my social media activity?
- What level of marketing activity can I sustain across all the platforms and options that may be valuable for my brand?

Digital Brand Footprint Hints

With those questions in mind, here are a few considerations about your digital brand footprint on two key sites: LinkedIn and Twitter.

LinkedIn

LinkedIn is a must have for any consultant now. It is used by more than 150 million people for networking and professional connections, so it is important to be there. Not only is it the first place a client will evaluate your skills, it is also the conduit to several of the digital platform sites; you join by providing them access to your profile. Given that fact, that means your profile can be part of several digital platforms, which is all the more reason why it should be perfect and complete. Here are some tips for looking good on LinkedIn.

1. **Have a picture.** When I see someone with just the blue avatar for a head, I immediately assume he or she is not an active LinkedIn user. As such, they are not really interested in the networking. Apparently I am not alone in this bias. You need a picture to be taken seriously.

2. **Use the right picture.** That said, it has to be the right picture. LinkedIn is a business site, so you should use a professional-looking photo that is current. The head shot cropped from what must have been a group shot that looks somewhat grainy just doesn't cut it. Similarly, a recreational shot of windsurfing or sipping chardonnay only works if you are in the active sports or wine and food domains, respectively.

3. **Complete your profile accurately.** Don't lie or exaggerate. You will be found out. At the same time, be complete. If you worked for a firm that is not well known, define it (e.g., "Smith and Jones, the largest digital advertising firm in Peoria"). Don't expect visitors to your profile to try to visit the firm's website to figure out what it does. Moreover, you don't want visitors leaving your page so quickly anyway.

4. **Use the title headline cleverly.** Every user has a title headline just below his or her name. Many people don't even use this additional real estate on the site. You have 120 characters to play with, so use them. Consider it a great way to broadcast your brand. For example, "John Smith, Expert in Supply Chain Management for Growing Technology Companies" is a lot better than "John Smith, Founder Smith Consulting."

5. **Only link to people with whom you have a connection.** Ideally you should only connect with those you know. That said, if your former coworker John can connect you to someone you want to meet, don't just use a generic invite message. Provide the back story so the contact knows that John was willing to make the introduction for you. Similarly, choose to accept link requests carefully. There are people who are linking in just to collect names. Unless you are a recruiter, you don't want to appear like one.

6. **Add a projects section to your profile.** Once you start getting gigs, include them as part of your profile. You can even have HTML link to the projects URL if there is one. You can also include the LinkedIn thumbnail of other people who may have worked with you on that project.

7. **Join groups.** According to LinkedIn, fewer than 16 percent of users join the maximum number of groups, which is 50. Being an active participant in groups is far more likely to get your profile noticed. Most consultants are likely to have a few groups in their area of expertise. Additionally, there are usually groups for alumni organizations as well. Also, if you are a member of a group, you need not have one of your contacts intervene to be able to message someone. As such, the LinkedIn network becomes more accessible the more groups you are in.

8. **Blog on LinkedIn.** LinkedIn recently established a blog platform. For most professionals without a website or blog, LinkedIn hoped to be the platform of choice. As for any blog, make sure the content is rich, keep headlines short, and be aware of your frequency. Again tout your thought leadership. Keep in mind, though, if you are blogging on another site, as I do on marionmcgovern.com, your blog posts when ported to LinkedIn will go in your update stream, not to the LinkedIn blog site. I have on occasion disconnected my Wordpress link to LinkedIn and reposted my entire blog post directly in LinkedIn. Again, it adds to the work, but it may make a post more visible to the LinkedIn community.

9. **Recognize that your LinkedIn endorsements are not meaningful.** It has happened to all of us; someone you barely know and have not worked with endorses you for a skill on LinkedIn. Although that endorsement may support the one from your cofounder, it is not based on knowledge. People seem to toss around endorsements, perhaps hoping that you will reciprocate and tout a skill for them. I find this practice belittles the entire exercise. It is not something that builds trust in your expertise, it is more like a "like" on Facebook. So perhaps it is nice if you have a lot of endorsements, but don't sweat it if you don't.

Catherine Fisher, Senior Director of Marketing at LinkedIn stresses that it is critical to interact regularly with the platform.[7] The biggest mistake people make, in her opinion, is not connecting on a regular basis with the community. LinkedIn is all about relationships, and they want users to use the platform to nurture those relationships.

Twitter

Twitter is the brand accessory for the time-challenged; why draft a whole blog when you can say something meaningful in 140 characters? Twitter is among the fastest-growing social media platforms,[8] so if you aren't tweeting, you may just want to jump in, because on Twitter you can share your point of view. You can tell your followers and hopefully potential customers how you feel about issues and developments in your industry. This is a channel that can build your credibility, so it could be well worth the effort to make it resonate. Here are some tips.

1. **Learn Twitter.** If you are a novice, figure it out. There are many Internet sites to assist you, from a course at Lynda.com to wiki sites. There is even a *Twitter for Dummies* book, so whatever learning mode is best for you, just do it. Once done, complete your profile.

2. **Build your consulting channel.** To build your brand as a consultant, you need to isolate the content that is out there in the Twitter universe to find the information most relevant to your practice, your client, and your brand. As such, you should create a list that amalgamates all those important tweeters, the experts in your industry and functional domain. I have a list just for this book of digital platform companies, freelance sites, independent contractor sites, and so forth. Every day I check it to see what is going on in the world of my book. I have other lists, too, including one for my humanitarian non-profit that sends reconstructive surgeons to the developing world. As you might surmise, there is no overlap between those lists. (That said, I probably have a lot of plastic surgeon followers who are wondering about my fascination with the Uber employment lawsuit.) Build the lists that matter for your brand so you can target the right content. But also build lists that help you stay current. I have a news list, in which I have all of my news sources from CNN to the *Guardian*. If I step off a plane

and my phone has been off, I can immediately check the head-lines. Similarly, I have a sports list, so I always know, even if I don't want to, how the San Francisco Giants are doing.

3. **Only share quality content.** I share the things I want to be known for, my thought leadership. That said, I also share topics across a realm of subjects that I find fascinating, provocative, and well-written. By sharing only very interesting stuff, you become a resource for content for your followers.

4. **Follow two new people each day.** You will need to work Twitter to get any type of result from it. One way is to identify two new people to follow every day. You can always choose one person from Twitter's "Who to Follow" tab. Don't forget to follow some fun people. Per above, I have a fun list in addition to my business one, in which I follow Bruce Springsteen, Ian Poulter, and KarltheFog, a digital proxy for the famous San Francisco fog.

5. **Reply to everything.** If people tweet to you or mention your tweet or like your tweet, thank them and or keep the conversation going. In fact, it is good to favorite any retweets you get. It's often good to get a conversation going. Always use the follower's handle, because that brings more people into the conversation.

6. **Follow back anyone who has followed you.** This is a good practice. That said, you do have some leeway. For some reason, an S&M maven in Sydney followed me. I did not follow her back.

7. **Discover and retweet at least two top items a day.** Twitter's "Discover" button is great to find tweets that may be of interest. It also helps you find resources that you may want to follow for more original content.

8. **Tweet at least two original tweets twice a day.** For some people this can be the hardest thing, but the more you do it, the more you will get comfortable with putting your point of view out there. The more original tweets you do, the more of a following you will get and the more you will become engaged with the platform. Use existing hashtags or make up your own, Remember: Hashtags help you be found.

As this section indicates, curating your digital brand is not without an amount of effort. That said, the effort could add tremendously to the brand you are building.

Digital Branding Control

Finally, you may want to ensure you have full oversight of your digital brand. For those who may have negative posts or an embarrassing online history, this could be essential. For most, it can just make good sense.

There are several companies that will manage your digital reputation as a cost, including Reputation.com, Reputation 911, and Gadook. Many are more focused on providing reputation management services for corporations and their brands, so if you want to consider using a service, be sure to evaluate the firm's expertise with individuals.

I am a user of BrandYourself.com, a DIY site that makes digital brand management affordable for individuals. You can get a free account or additional service at a fairly low cost. It scans the web to identify what information is out there about a given person. For people with common names, such as Mary Smith, this could bring up many citations and make for a difficult sifting process. I was shocked to find that there was a former state police commander in Pennsylvania named Marian McGovern (a different spelling, but nonetheless a potential source of confusion) as well as an obituary for another Marion McGovern. I indicated on the site which of the citations found were me and which were not.

Potential clients and employers are googling you not just to see your experience, but also to find any "red flags" about you. Any indication that you may be difficult to work with, such as a derisive tweet, could end the interaction before it begins. It is for this reason that many users of these sorts of sites are independent professionals who know they need to protect their digital reputations.

If there are negative items, whether posts, comments, or pictures, the site leads you through a process to mute those. By making more current and more positive things more prominent in a Google search, the negative items become effectively suppressed. I revisit periodically just to check on my digital brand.

A Final Word on the Digital World

Maintaining your digital brand takes some work and could result in an inordinate time being spent at your computer screen curating your image. Don't fall into a trap of thinking that, just by serving things up digitally, you are advancing your practice. You may be, but keep in mind that people buy from people who have authentic expertise. In fact, the Solo Project, an effort that researched the lives of independent workers or Soloists, had a key finding about social media in its Solo City Report: "Social media is useless."[9] They were referring to its value as a source of business rather than a branding tool, citing the fact that only 4 percent of those they surveyed thought it was a valuable source of business. So keep that in mind: It's good for branding, but not sales. You need to be out working in the field, attending conferences, meeting people, and making personal connections on a regular basis.

Consulting is a profession. Many professions, including education, law, and medicine, require continuing education to remain certified. You should be doing your own continuing education to build your brand. And though online courses might seem an easy option, be sure to spend time meeting people and making connections in person, so you can enhance your own expertise.

Chapter 4 Key Takeaways

- Your brand is based on your core values.
- Techniques to refine your consulting brand include a values screen, SWOT analysis, and a positioning statement exercise.
- Any text associated with your brand should be perfect, with no spelling or grammar errors.
- Any information provided about your background should be accurate and unembellished.
- Social media channels can help build personal brands, but which to choose depends on your specialty.
- LinkedIn and Twitter should be curated by most consultants as brand-building sites.
- Recognize that brand building with social media will take regular time and attention.

- You may want to invest in a digital brand-reputation tool to have more control over your online brand.

- Digital brand building via social media channels is not a way to generate sales but a way to enhance your sales efforts.

5

The Price Is Right

Now that you have defined your value proposition, built and enraptured your brand, and begun curating the digital voice of that brand, it's time to begin selling your ideas and yourself. Ten years ago, the path ahead of you would have had a much longer-term horizon. You would have hung up your shingle, as the saying goes, and started personal selling and networking. Now in the social media age, things can happen much more quickly. That said, you still need to pursue multiple paths to build a successful practice.

> "Show me the money."
>
> —Rod Tidwell
> *Jerry Maguire*

But first things first. It's time to talk money.

Fee Structures

Fees are set in many ways, but there are four broad categories: an hourly fee, a project fee, a success fee, and an equity deal. The first is by far the most common; companies are used to paying professional services providers, such as lawyers and accountants, by the hour, so paying a consultant the same way is logical. That said, it is important to understand the legal implications of hourly rates because, depending on the nature of the work being done, there could be legal issues due to wage and hour infractions. Moreover, some regulators see an hourly fee as a red flag, indicating that the individual should be considered an employee rather than a contractor. (We will cover this subject in Chapter 7.)

There are many resources available to help create the formula for your daily rate, taking into account the time you expect to be earning, the time that will be unbillable either due to vacations or business development time, expenses from marketing costs to accounting fees, and target income before taxes. The website ConsultingSuccess.com has an online tool for the calculations. The result, however, must be calibrated against what clients may be willing to pay for your services.

Per diems are daily extensions of an hourly rate. Some clients prefer this method, especially if they are concerned about the number of hours that may be worked in a day. This is also a popular method for workshop facilitators and strategy consultants. Because strategic planning sessions or training sessions tend to only last a few days, pricing the gig at $2,000/day, for example, can be a more effective pricing approach.

Similarly, monthly billing on a retainer basis is a natural extrapolation of an hourly fee and appropriate for situations in which the amount of time required per month may be uncertain or variable. The retainer is typically for a less-than-full-time commitment. Small firms that may engage a part time CFO on a contract basis, for example, may be more comfortable with a retainer structure. Retainers are especially common in the public relations field. One issue with a retainer, though, is that a client may ask more of you then can be completed in the time allotted. The best way to structure the retainer to ensure a fair price is to define a "not to exceed" level of hours in a given period. Additional hours beyond that level can be purchased at a mutually agreed upon hourly rate.

Project fees are the norm in the strategy and technology realms. Consultants who choose this method must be adept at estimating their costs and especially the time required to achieve the desired result. If you use this, you must be clear about the deliverables from the onset. The bane of existence for many consultants who bill by the project is "scope creep," which happens when a client continually asks for work not envisioned in the original project definition. It is up to the consultant to ensure work that may not be part of the agreement is either deferred or renegotiated as a separate contract.

Many large companies, such as Cisco Systems, have recognized this issue from the other side. They feel they don't always get the results for which they believe they are contracting. Consequently, they have leveraged project management methodologies and developed sophisticated "Statements of Work" (SOW) formats with detailed deliverables.

A SOW is a standard in most project management programs, where in companies contract for the delivery of discrete parts of projects. The Statement of Work outlines the details of the efforts. The fact that Staffing Industry Analysts included SOW-based projects as one of its categories of independent work in its recent study, "Measuring the Gig Economy: Inside the New Paradigm of Contingent Work," illustrates the growing adoption of this approach. A well-drafted SOW will include:

- A project description or scope of work.
- Deliverables including a detailed description of each and due dates.
- Schedule and any scheduling issues that can be foreseen (i.e., holidays or access to certain people, reports or resources).
- Location where the work will be performed.
- Reporting of both interim and final deliverables.
- Fees, including allowable expenses.

Fees are typically done on a milestone basis. Many SOW projects are long, so deliverable-based billing is often supplemented with a monthly retainer. Most companies working with SOWs have sophisticated project tracking systems. Typically, achievement of a deliverable triggers payment of fees. Consultants working in these environments need to understand the intricacies of these systems to ensure the accuracy of their reporting and the success of their engagements.

Success fees are typically for financing or M&A gigs; a consultant is paid for his or her performance in securing funding or a buyer for a company. In a success fee, the financial consultant would get a percentage of the sales price or money raised. More sophisticated firms may use a reverse Lehman structure, in which the percentage that determines the fee is higher the more money is raised.

Another success fee application is in operational improvement projects, in which the fee is determined by virtue of the savings achieved through the engagement. The challenge in these situations is identifying the savings directly attributable to the project. There must be clarity before the fact on how the calculations will be made to determine the compensable savings.

Finally, equity can be king in the startup world. If you choose this option, understand it is the riskiest, because the firm value may never be liquid. Also, even though it is not liquid, it has a value when awarded. As such, the $5,000 you receive in ABC startup stock will still be something you will need to report as taxable income. As such, it is best to combine warrants or stock with some cash compensation at least to cover the tax burden. In my M Squared days, our CFO would need to approve any equity in lieu of fees, because it was in essence a credit decision; he evaluated the financial stability of the firm before we did the deal. Be sure to consult your tax advisor and perhaps your accountant if considering equity fees.

Setting the Price

Once you know the structure of your engagement fees, then consider how much you will charge. One thing many consultants fail to consider is that the work—not your expertise, fee schedule, or pedigree—determines the price. An individual can and should have a range of fees. An interim CFO stepping into a bankruptcy crisis should charge more than he/she would stepping in to develop a financing plan for a subsidiary. Similarly, work you secure from a referral may warrant a lower fee, because it required less effort to obtain. What is most important, though, is the market price.

The idea of a market price for consulting work will invariably rub some readers the wrong way. Consultants are not commodities, unlike traditional office temps, so how can there be a market price? Potentially, the advent of digital platforms will create a frictionless market in which a true market price can emerge.

Right now, though, the best analogy is housing. Anyone who has ever bought or sold a house understands the notion of "comparables." No two houses are exactly the same, so realtors use comparables to set the listing price. One comparable may have a pool, whereas another may have a tree house—attributes that will be valued differently in the calculation. The same is true with consulting. No two projects are alike and the skill brought to bear on them differ as well. Even pedigrees differ; the emphasis of an MBA from the University of Chicago will vary significantly from the program at Stanford or Yale.

And of course, one key comparable to consider is what the price would be to hire someone as an employee to do the work. Another likely substitute is what it would cost to hire a brand-name consulting firm such as McKinsey or a specialized one such as Bridgespan.

So factor all of those comparables when you want to establish your price range. Here are some other things to consider when setting your price:

- **Risk and return are directly correlated.** The riskier a project, whether due to the scope or aggressive goals, the more it should pay. Turnaround situations are a case in point. The potential for failure is high so the rewards should be as well. Similarly, if a project is very low risk for you, because you have done something similar a thousand times, then a lower fee may be warranted.

- **Capital formation is a long-term investment.** If an engagement is going to build your intellectual capital by broadening your skill base, you should be willing to do it for less than you might otherwise. This is because in the long run, you become more marketable and potentially can command higher fees. Consider it an investment in your practice. As an aside, some people have taken this to an extreme, by offering to do certain experientially expansive projects for free. Aside from pro bono work for a not-for-profit, I would not recommend such a practice. A lower fee makes sense, but zero fee diminishes the effort.

    Conversely, if a client wants you for your unique knowledge of an industry, company, or technology, and plans to own and/or exploit the intellectual property you bring to the engagement, you should charge a higher price. You need more of a return on your investment.

- **Sometimes you need hazard pay.** Hazard pay is typical in very dangerous assignments, such as security contracts at U.S. embassies in dangerous countries. But sometimes a consulting engagement can be hazardous as well. We once worked on a forensic accounting project for a hospital system that had used outdated tax tables to run end of year payroll at all 25 of its hospitals. As such, 25 CEOs had been improperly paid. It wasn't a pretty picture. That gig commanded a premium, as it was not only tedious, but fraught with conflict and extremely high profile as well.

- **Uber rides and rental cars charge differently.** Denis Russel, the coauthor of my first book, *A New Brand of Expertise*, had a great pricing analogy for consultants that compared the difference between cabs and rental cars.[1] Given the title of this book, I have updated the metaphor to be Uber services. The idea is that people use both Uber cars and rental cars for different purposes. The Uber car charges much more per mile than the rental car, because it is a short stint with convenience and urgency at a premium. Similarly, a client who wants something yesterday, versus one who is open to a three-month study, should have very different pricing algorithms.

- **The 1-percent rule helps.** Again, in my first book, I mention this handy rule of thumb.[2] A person's daily fee should be 1 percent of his or her equivalent annualized salary. A marketing consultant who feels $200K would be the going rate for her expertise should then charge $2,000 per day for her services, or $250 per hour. A more junior person who could command $80K per year should charge $800 per day, or $100 per hour. That said, though, keep in mind it is the work, not your pedigree that should determine the price.

- **Anchor clients deserve a deal.** In real estate, they refer to the primary retailer in a mall as the anchor tenant. Not only are they bringing in the shoppers, they are paying a significant portion of the rent. An anchor client is one that pays your rent, so to speak, by giving you recurring business. Having that project year in and year out from that one client is a wonderful thing. Some consultants may want to increase the fees after a few years. Unless your costs have risen dramatically as well, resist that impulse. Being able to plan your year with a known piece of work on the books is a luxury for some, and one that should be managed carefully.

- **Government contracting is not for the faint of heart.** The federal government and state governments are among the largest consumers of consulting services. The General Services Administration spends about $50 billion annually, much of it ear marked for small businesses. However, doing business with the government as an independent is not easy. No surprises there. To be eligible to win government contracts, you will first need to obtain through Dunn & Bradstreet a D-U-N-S number, a unique nine-digit number. In many cases, you may need a security clearance. You will also need to register with the System for Award Management (SAM). If this seems a bit complicated, that is because it is.

One option for those who are expert in the areas sought by the government is to align yourself with smaller consulting firms that may be in need of your services. That firm would go through the tedious process with the government and you wouldn't have to.

Chapter 5 Key Takeaways

- There are many different types of fees structures.
- Pricing depends not just on your skills and expertise, but on the nature of the work.
- Statement of Work–based projects are becoming more prevalent especially in the technology sector. Pricing in these cases is based on deliverables.
- Government contracting may require affiliation with another firm or employment platform.

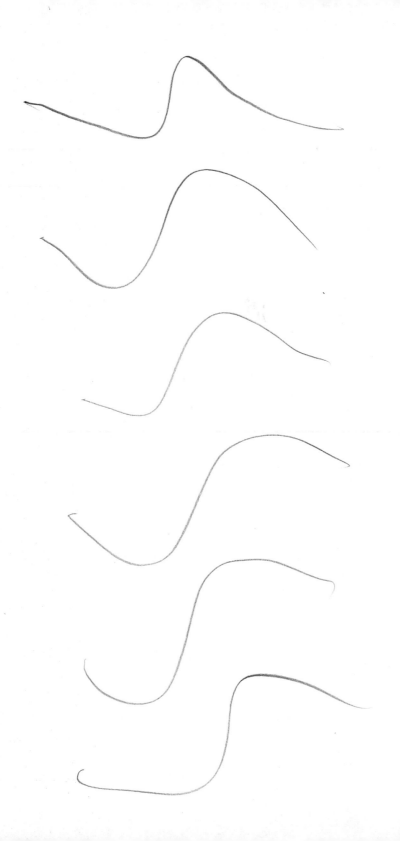

6

Selling in the New Marketplace

Launching Your Practice

Some people have the *Field of Dreams* mantra when they start consulting: "If I build it, they will come." But the truth of the matter is that selling consulting services even for the best-in-class experts takes a continuous, focused effort. There are three main approaches to consider:

1. Personal direct sales.
2. Working through an intermediary or specialty consulting firm.
3. Working through a digital talent platform.

> "Ninety percent of selling is conviction and ten percent is persuasion."
> —Shiv Khera

Direct Sales

Some people love to sell and others don't. Some people love to sell products, but hate to sell themselves. As part of the research for this book, I did a survey of independent consultants that focused on how they run their practices. Fewer than 5 percent of respondents said they loved the selling part of running their business. Forty percent said they did it because they had to.

The key to being able to sell is believing in the product. If you really believe you can deliver results to clients, then sales will follow. For seasoned consultants, this is the most common way to get business.

The steps are the same as for any product: lead generation, cultivation, and qualification followed by an ask. Lead generation can be anything from sending out an email newsletter to networking at the professional association of your industry.

Cultivation can be through blog posts or thought leadership white papers. Thought leadership, by the way, was one of the favorite tasks consultants cited in my survey. Qualification is the crucial step of determining whether a potential project is not only real (i.e. has a budget and a degree of urgency), but is appropriate for your expertise. The ask is the all-important throwing of your hat into the ring and submitting a bid or proposal for the work. Resources abound to provide assistance in this area, from websites such as ConsultingSuccess.com to the industry association the Institute of Management Consulting.

When you sell directly to clients, you are in total control of your destiny; you choose the clients to target and the types of projects to pursue. As such, you are in control of the brand promise you defined for your practice.

Similarly, in collaboration with your client, you negotiate your own price, contractual provisions, and time frame. This presupposes you have the infrastructure to handle all of those things. Operating independently requires more organization and structure. You will need a basic contract, accounting system (or at least invoicing tool), and some level of administrative support (a topic we will cover in Chapter 8).

From the marketing standpoint, direct sales is the most time-consuming. Although many consultants begin their careers with a project in hand from a former employer or old friend, those who do not need to mine their contacts to generate leads, network whenever and wherever they can to cultivate relationships, and cleverly generate opportunities to sell work. Although social media tools such as LinkedIn help to facilitate the work of marketing through contacts, it still takes a concerted effort on your part. (As I mentioned in Chapter 4, social media is not a sales strategy.)

It may take many lunches, attendance at networking events, and/or speaking engagements before you secure good leads for your business. Let's face it: many people don't like networking, but a recent survey by

Cerius Executives, an intermediary in Los Angeles, found that most senior consultants secured nearly 85 percent of their business through networking.[1] With those kinds of numbers, it is a step you can't ignore and something you should think about strategically.

This investment in business development is a cost of doing business. That cost is not just the dollars expended in attending a conference, it is also the opportunity cost of your time; the time you spend marketing is time spent not generating income-producing work. Although all sales channels have unbillable time, direct sales may have the highest level, especially for rookie consultants. This is why many people, both veterans and rookies, turn to intermediaries to add more momentum to their own sales efforts.

Using Traditional Intermediaries

Intermediaries can provide you with opportunities you might not encounter on your own, but you take the risk that the projects may not be the optimal content for your skills. Similarly, the price point may not be at the rate you have set for your services and so may not be right for your economic situation. Nonetheless, it can be a solid sales strategy.

Specialty consulting firms, such as McKinley Marketing and the Business Talent Group, operate on the value proposition that deploying independent consulting expertise is a critical business strategy. They work with clients to help them understand ways they can tap this just-in-time marketplace for competitive advantage. The consultant's benefit from the firm's reputation as a problem-solver. These firms are not selling a consultant individually, but they are selling the fact that they can find the right expert to solve the problem. In essence, consultants working through these firms are leveraging the firm's brand to help burnish their own.

When you work through a specialty firm, they will secure a project through their sales team and contact you if they think you are a fit for it. The project typically has a budget that the firm has negotiated with the client. That budget may or may not be in line with the pricing you have established for your business. You need to decide whether or not to put your hat in the ring for consideration.

There are several reasons why you should consider a lower fee when working through an intermediary:

- A project may afford the opportunity to add new skills to your repertoire. Perhaps you have been a digital marketing specialist with a domestic consumer brand, and a project comes up for a digital strategist for that same product category in key international markets. The ability to add the international skill to your own inventory of skills is worth a lower rate. (As I mentioned in Chapter 5, capital formation is worth the investment.)

- You had little or no sales expense associated with securing this project. As such, you should be willing to reduce the fee you might charge in your direct sales channel.

- It could be a company for whom you always wanted to work. Back in the day, M Squared did a great deal of work with Lucas Films and Lucas Digital. Several projects were out at Skywalker Ranch, which is approximately 45 minutes from San Francisco in the middle of nowhere (literally—directions to the ranch included the dirt road one used at a certain mileage point to find the unmarked location). An inordinate number of consultants were willing to reduce fees and commute for these opportunities.

Most firms check references specific for a given engagement. To optimize your dealings with them, you should have such references organized. A marketing communications consultant with diverse clients, for example, should be able to easily offer references specific for a speech-writing gig versus an annual report project.

The intermediary firm typically handles the invoicing and collection of funds from the client. Similarly, the firm deals with the contracts and insurance requirements. Some will allow you to negotiate specific provisions in your contract; however, recognize that they have a contract with the buyer that mirrors the contract with you. As such, major deviations from the standard contract may not be negotiable on the client side. (We will discuss these issues more in Chapter 8.)

What many consultants like the most, though, is that these firms have sales forces. Their sales teams are out in the marketplace selling the idea of specialized expertise to clients. By doing this, they are potentially presenting you with projects from companies you don't know, projects you would never have secured on your own. However, because they are selling solutions, they are not necessarily selling you. It could be that the projects they secure are not a fit for your expertise. The firms typically have a broad reach with a client, so are reluctant to turn away qualified consultants. So even though they accepted you into their network, it doesn't mean they will secure you a gig.

To ensure the best fit with the intermediary world, you should be careful and deliberate in choosing the intermediaries for your practice. Some are appropriate only for those in certain functional areas, such as CFOs to Go; others may only assist consultants at a certain level of the organization, such as the Association of Interim Executives, which cultivates only the most senior interim management consultants. Many are only regional in focus, such as McKinley Marketing in Washington, D.C., whereas others may be offshoots of large human capital or staffing organizations.

This space can be confusing, as firms may identify themselves as specialty consulting firms, staffing companies, or high-end temporary agencies. The true intermediary recognizes that it has two clients: the customers who need expertise and the consultants who are seeking engagements. Because the firm acts as a marketing arm for those consultants it represents, it must have the commensurate level of sophistication and industry knowledge to sell the services of its network. You are the subject matter expert, so the intermediary need not have your level of expertise, but they need to be able to hold their own in your field. As you interact with each firm, assess its familiarity with your industry segment to see if they can adequately market you.

Here are some other points for you to consider:

- **How core is professional level business to the firm?** The value of the intermediary is its ability to bring senior-level engagements to you. If it's merely an outgrowth of a traditional staffing firm, it may not have this expertise. Moreover, its support structures and sales incentives may not be geared to secure the types of assignments of interest to senior consultants.

- **Has the intermediary had projects in the past for which you would have been a fit?** The past can be a predictor of the future. If you are looking for senior-level compensation program design work, then make sure it has done those projects in the past.

- **What is the organizational heritage of the firm?** Most intermediaries have background in staffing, search, or consulting.

Firms with roots in consulting or search often have a higher service orientation and may be more familiar with the decision processes of senior-level buyers.

- **How does the firm define its services?** Language can be a very telling indicator of positioning in the intermediary marketplace. High-end intermediaries focus on the solutions they delivered to client problems rather than the number of placements they have made. The following illustrates some terms that can be bellwether indicators of a firm's leaning:

Intermediary Language

High End Firm   Others

High End Firm	Others
Engagement	Job Order

| Consultant | Contractor |

| Fee | Pay Rate |

- **What services does the firm provide to you?** Service levels vary across the industry. Some firms make the match, set the prices, and negotiate the contract with little or no interaction with the consultant. Others have a more interactive process. Which would feel better to you?

- **How good are they at solving client problems?** Every firm has its own "secret sauce" that helps it make the right match of consultants for client projects. Some, such as M Squared, rely on a highly sophisticated project specification process that forces clients to distill key issues and desired outcomes. Some firms go beyond skill-set matching but also consider essential soft skills. Cerius Executives in Los Angeles includes a psychometric profiling process for all consultants it accepts in its networks. Client projects are similarly profiled in order to use predictive analytics to facilitate the best possible behavioral match.

- **How sophisticated is their operating infrastructure?** In most cases, you will be using the intermediary's system to bill the client. How easy, comprehensive, and suitable is that? If you do SOW-based projects and bill by deliverables, can its system handle that? Does it have an app to make it easy for you to report your progress? If yes, is that something you care about and would use? Do they offer guidelines and support for expense reporting?

- **How will you be compensated?** We will cover employment issues in Chapter 7, but it is important to know whether you will be employed by the intermediary or the client, or working on your own and paid using a 1099. If you are being paid by the intermediary, it is important to understand its financial stability. By law, as an employee, you need to be paid within a 14-day window following completion of the pay cycle. The client may not pay for 30, 60, or even 90 days. As such, the intermediary must fund that receivable and pay you before payment is received.

- **Are benefits of any sort available?** The Affordable Care Act (ACA) has meant that many intermediaries need not offer health insurances. (The future of the ACA is now up in the air, a topic we will discuss in Chapter 10.) Several firms offer benefit opportunities for things that are difficult for an independent consultant to procure, such as long-term care insurance coverage. Some have paid time off plans prorated for the days worked by a consultant on an assignment. You should understand what would be available to you, were you to work with a particular firm and how important that is to you.

There are many great intermediary firms in the talent space. It is worth your while to find the one or ones who can best help you build your business.

Digital Talent Platforms

Digital talent platforms are a relatively new phenomenon, so it is difficult to get a sense of the volume of work that is actually being facilitated through this channel. This is especially true because most of the analytics that have been done have included the on-demand platforms of ride-sharing companies such as Uber and lower-skill providers such as TaskRabbit. A highly regarded study in the field done in 2015 by JP Morgan Chase showed very low levels of participation in the on-demand labor platforms of about .5 percent of American workers. Nonetheless, the study and several others concluded that these platforms are growing at a healthy clip, increasing ten-fold over a three-year period.[2] There are a plethora of platforms across a variety of skill sets, like consultants, drivers, designers, teachers and coaches. Appendix A provides a listing of many of these companies, as well as selected traditional intermediaries.

The JP Morgan Chase study also concluded that participants in on-demand labor platforms used them to supplement primary income streams. As such, it is worth considering these firms as a way to find work that might not come from the other channels, rather than as a sole source of clients.

Although they may seem similar, digital talent platforms operate differently from traditional intermediaries. The biggest difference is that you need to invest time and effort to secure gigs.

While writing this book, I applied to every platform for which I was seemingly qualified. I wanted to better understand the application process as well as the user experience. Appendix B provides a table of my experiences with some of the platforms I joined. My opinion is that an investment of time is required to make any of the platforms generate appropriate projects for you. This is due in part to their algorithmic operation. An algorithm may suggest you are good for project X, but it will not know for sure unless you are selected or in some cases, considered, for project X. In other words, the system cannot be smarter about what is right for you, unless it has more data about what projects you have applied for and the outcome of those applications.

Once you join, you need to work the platform, and you need to figure out what project might work for you. Most allow you to respond to a project posting with the reasons why you may be a good fit for it. Some even give you templates from your prior submissions, so you don't have to keep generating unique responses to posted projects.

The pricing content of these responses differs across platforms as well. In some, you immediately provide a price at which you will do the work; in others, there is more of an iterative process, in which you interact with the buyer to get more details to facilitate the setting of an appropriate fee.

PROFILE: EXPERFY

Experfy is a digital talent platform that specializes in data scientists. It was launched by the Harvard Innovation Labs to much fanfare in 2014, because it was clearly addressing an evolving need: a shortage of data scientists. A 2013 McKinsey report noted that in the near future, there will be a shortage of 1.5 million managers who understand how to interpret data, while at the same time, the level of data will be doubling on a regular basis.

The press it received (it was a favorite at Tech Crunch) led to an influx of candidates—20,000. It only accepted about 3,300. It has a rigorous application and vetting process that includes looking not only at LinkedIn profiles, but also Kaggle accounts, assessing how candidates have done in various Kaggle competitions. (Kaggle competitions are data scientist hackathons.)

Clients are Fortune 500 and mid-sized firms. They are typically in data intensive industries, retail, advertising, travel, ecommerce. Healthcare is a little slow but it's coming. The buyer is typically the chief innovation officer, the chief data scientist, or the chief analytics officer. CMOs and marketing departments are also clients.

COO Harpreet Singh notes that Experfy considers itself a technology company, not a human capital one. It looks forward to having its platform power more marketplaces for hosted analytics of other sorts. He believes the need for marketplaces will continue as the freelancing trend continues. There is a cultural change going on that is accelerating this. He does believe his people see themselves as gig workers, albeit very highly paid ones, averaging $250 per hour.

Because such an investment of time is needed to make it work, it is important to choose the right digital platform. Many of the questions you needed to consider about a traditional intermediary apply here as well.

- **How core is professional level business to the firm?** When you check out the platform, see where your brand of expertise fits in the array of services it offers. Although Upwork maintains it works with senior consultants, given that so much of its business is on lower-level programming and creative disciplines, I would not see them as a fruitful channel to secure serious consulting engagements in management disciplines.

- **Has it filled gigs for which you would have been a fit?** This can sometimes be difficult to ascertain. Some sites cater to a specific managerial discipline, such as SpareHire, which is focused primarily on financial expertise as well as quantitative marketing analysis. The majority, though, are more general. What you can do on most sites is browse their current opportunities. If some of those seem relevant or interesting to you, it might be worth the application time. Keep in mind that the most popular projects on these sites are ones that can largely be done remotely. As such, the majority of gigs listed are business plans, market or product studies, and research projects. If you are an organizational consultant, for example, your project opportunities may be fewer and further between. Similarly, operations and manufacturing gigs are not widely represented.

- **How will it determine whether you have the right expertise?** Groucho Marx once said he wouldn't want to join a club that would take him as a member. Who are the other "members of the club" you are considering? Can anybody join, or is there some gatekeeper? Touting a network of 50,000 consultants is meaningless if many of them are low-level, unqualified, or potentially fictitious. Although a vetting process may seem to be an onerous burden, it can be a sign of a more exclusive club, and one that you may want to join. Here are some examples:

Hourly Nerd/Catalant—Must have an MBA from a "top" school.

GLG—Must take an online confidentiality course.

Experfy—Must have a Kaggle score of a certain number.

UpCounsel—Must be a lawyer in only certain specialties.

ExecRank—Must complete an onboarding session.

Perhaps the most rigorous vetting process may be TopTal, a platform which purports to have only the top 3 percent of the freelance talent in the disciplines of designers, software developers, and financial expertise. Its website (TopTal.com) explains how it gets to the top 3 percent, which as illustrated here:

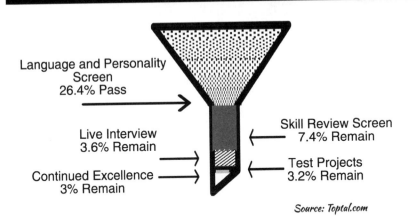

TopTal Vetting Process

Language and Personality Screen
26.4% Pass

Live Interview
3.6% Remain

Continued Excellence
3% Remain

Skill Review Screen
7.4% Remain

Test Projects
3.2% Remain

Source: Toptal.com

- **How does it make money?** The platform world is still evolving, so there are multiple business models being developed. Like traditional intermediaries, platforms have two clients: the consultants and the companies. As such, how the platform makes money must suit both types of participants. Most platforms take a percentage of the project fee. Some subsidize one side of the platform with the other (i.e., they charge the consultants to increase revenues). ExecRank is a platform targeted at board-level advisors on one side, and start-ups and mezzanine-level firms on the other. The advisors pay a monthly fee to be included in the cadre of experts. I must admit, I pay more attention to this platform, because I am paying for it. That said, I have received more targeted and appropriate opportunities for my skill set from ExecRank than I have from any other platform.

- **What services does the platform offer?** Some platforms offer additional services to participants. Chief among these are training programs. Many of the Experfy participants, for example, are academics in the field, so they are more than able to provide online training content for the platform. Some, such as ExecRank, offer the opportunity to become certified in some way in particular fields. Many platforms offer access to helpful resources including tax planning guides or incorporation services. Some have blogging platforms to help you build your brand among their participants. Perhaps the most unique might be Tongal, which is a platform for independent creative artists to power content for brands on you tube and in advertising. For the last three years, they have hosted the Tongies, an Academy Awards–like gathering to showcase the best work in various creative categories, such as long-form video or animation, done by those on its platform.

It is important to remember that digital platforms have two sides: both clients and consultants are members. So unlike the specialty consulting firm intermediary, from which you may not know immediately who the client is, you typically have optics into that on a digital platform. That said, the platform companies that have created these marketplaces need to protect their investment, so they have significant contracts to outline the relationships of the parties.

Unlike the online contract you get when you update your mobile phone software without ever reading the agreement, it is important to actually print out and read the agreement of the digital platforms on which you choose to participate. You may even need to secure some legal advice on certain parts of it. Although I have not read every single platform contract, I have read many, and here are some common points:

1. Typically, you and the client sign the same document. In fact, in order to apply to most platforms, you agree to the contract, which is why some people won't read it. (**Don't make that mistake!**)

2. The platform disavows responsibility for making the match, because participants on both sides of the platform make it happen. Similarly, the platform takes no responsibility for whether a given consultant has the requisite skills he or she has represented that will enable successful completion of the engagement.

3. Most platforms forbid participants from contacting each other outside of the platform. Emails and phone numbers cannot be shared. When I built my website using a developer from Fiverr, we were conversing about issues on the platform, and David, my programmer in Morocco, suggested we do a Skype call. When I messaged back with the words "my Skype ID," the screen immediately went red and let me know I may be in breach of contract. Suffice it to say, the platforms take the external contact restriction seriously. Given that my project did not go flawlessly and more direct communications would have been helpful, I was not a fan of this restriction.

4. Most put the onus for the decision as to whether a consultant is an employee or an independent contractor on the client. However, consultants should understand that many clients, especially startups and small and mid-sized companies, may not be equipped to make the right call on this issue. As such, it behooves you to understand the implications of the employment status decision. (We will discuss this more in Chapter 7.)

5. Payment practices are outlined. Most require invoicing to be through the platform, but some, such as SpareHire, are only now developing that capability. Most only take credit card payments from clients, although some are adjusting their models to accommodate other modes. Experfy, which works primarily with very large clients, does accept corporate purchase orders and corporate checks. In some cases, payment is made up-front when a gig commences and placed in escrow

until the project is completed. If the work you do tends to be long term, you need to understand how the payment process will work and whether it meets your cash flow needs.

6. Dispute resolution processes are also described. If the client is not satisfied with the work, he or she may not accept the project, meaning the funds may never be released to you the consultant. In most cases, the consultant can issue a dispute if he or she feels payment is due. This happened to me with one of my ill-fated Fiverr gigs. Suffice it to say, it is very important that you understand how disputes, especially those involving finished work, are resolved.

7. Most contracts address intellectual property (IP) ownership. We will discuss this more in Chapter 8, but if you are in a field where you want to own the IP you build, platform contracts may or may not enable that. Another of my Fiverr developers, the one who fixed things, created a specialty SEO optimization manual for me, so that I could optimize my blog posts without his involvement. Technically, that manual would be considered "work for hire" and I would own the right to that manual. He copyrighted the material, which was just fine with me, as I would have offered him a free, perpetual license, to enable him to use the document with other clients.

Once you have identified the platforms that play to your strengths and you have read the contracts, you need to apply to a subset of them. As I said, a time investment is needed. However, so is diversification. Right now, especially in the consulting platform space, there are a number of competitors. It is almost reminiscent of 2001, when there were five Internet pet food delivery services; it was clear to everyone that they would not all survive. In fact, a recent article in *Harvard Business Review* suggested that the digital platforms are not disrupting traditional businesses so much as they are forcing out similar but less efficient competitors.[3] To ensure you don't put all your platform eggs in one proverbial basket, apply to two or three of the set you find most interesting.

Working the Digital Platforms

Although they all work somewhat differently, here are some guidelines about how to optimize your possibility for jobs in the platform world.

- **Read everything on the site.** Virtually all platforms have a blog, where at least some of the postings are targeted at the consultant side of the platform. There is bound to be a post about how best to work with the firm. Other typical content includes codes of conduct, reference guidelines, and employment status information. Take it all in and follow their guidelines.

- **Join the extracurriculars.** Some sites will have special networking groups of consultants from like industries. They may call them advisory networks or expert councils. Even if you don't feel completely expert, join the group that best matches your expertise and work that as well. Read the posts, hear about the projects other members completed, and attend webcasts that support your expertise. Some platforms even make suggestions of other members with whom you should network. Another approach is a program recently launched by Catalant/Hourly Nerd called Project Ideas. With this tool, you can promote gigs that you could do for clients. Theoretically, the platform will then market those projects to its client community. The firm says clients often don't know what the consultant network can do, so this new feature is intended to showcase it. It doesn't hurt to try. That said, they have accepted my pitch for a training program about enhancing board governance, but as of yet, I have had no takers.

- **Define your bidding strategy.** When you bid, consider how a project fits with the brand you have defined for yourself. Also consider the practical dimensions:

  - Is the pay sufficient?

  - Do I have the time and can I meet a posted deadline?

  - Would I want to work for this type of client?

  - Are there any non-negotiables? (Non-negotiables are things that, because you are working for yourself, you just won't do, such as fly on a Sunday night. It could also be industries you wouldn't want to work in, such as porn or tobacco.)

- And then of course, the key question: Do I really have the right expertise and approach to meet the client's needs? Do not accept a gig that is over your head, regardless of how cool it may be. As a consultant once said to me, "You are only as good as your last gig," so don't take one that will reflect badly on you.

- **Develop a bidding plan and execute it.** At some point, you just need to jump in, but do so methodically. Develop a schedule of browsing projects once a week or more and set a goal of how many projects you will consider. Again, this will be a more successful approach for those in market research or strategy, as these projects are more popular on the platforms. That said, a strategy consultant could set a goal of bidding on three projects per week. Most platforms provide information including how long the gig has been open and how many bids have been received. Because you will be doing this across the two or three platforms you have chosen to join, you can also track your yield from each platform. Compare the following:

  - Your interview rate (# of interviews/# of bids).

  - Your win rate (# of gigs secured/# of bids).

  - The service level: Did I find out what happened with my bids (e.g., that it was filled by someone else), or did I remain in limbo, not knowing the ultimate disposition of the project or my proposal?

Comparing this data could help you determine whether a particular platform is the right channel to help you grow your business.

Chapter 6 Key Takeaways

- To launch your practice, you will need to pursue direct sales, which can be enhanced using a traditional intermediary and participating in digital platforms.

- There are many intermediaries, both traditional and digital, and you will need to screen them to understand which players are best to advance your practice.

- Traditional intermediaries sell consulting services and can secure projects for you that you might not get on your own.

- You will need to invest time to get a return from participating in digital platforms. Developing performance metrics may help you evaluate the best platform for you.

- Digital platforms may be best for marketing and strategy consultants who work off site on compartmentalized projects.

7

The Nasty Little Employment Problem

When it comes down to it, it is all about taxes. Whether we work as a manager for a Fortune 500 company, an independent PR consultant, a programmer on a digital platform, or a plumber, the income we generate is subject to federal and often state income tax. The remittance of that tax to the "feds" is contingent on the way in which we earn it and our corresponding employment status. As such, the government has a high level of interest in the question of whether you are an employee or not. Anyone who wants to thrive in the Gig Economy needs to understand the legal environment surrounding employment, especially the independent contractor vs. employee issue, but also the potential for wage and hour violations as well.

> "If you can't explain it simply, you don't understand it well enough."
> —Albert Einstein

For those in the human resources field, employment lawyers, or former CFOs who may have had to wrestle with these issues, feel free to skip to the next chapter. For those who feel up on the subject because you have followed the Uber independent contractor lawsuits, read on, for there are many nuances to consider and, of course, the jury is still out on those legal actions. So before we dive into the nitty gritty of employment law, let's look at one of the highest-profile employment cases in the last several years, the question of whether Uber drivers are employees or contractors.

An Overview of the 1099–W2 Debate

The current quagmire facing Uber about whether their drivers are independent contractors (ICs) or employees is a great development for the Gig Economy, as it may actually generate more awareness of the issue and potentially some solutions to what is a long-standing problem in the American workplace. This independent contractor compliance problem is not at all a new issue, but the actions involving one of the most high-profile unicorn companies has heightened the level of the discussion dramatically.

I have been following this case more closely than most people, because I have had the same problem, but on a smaller scale. In fact, when the news of the Uber lawsuit first broke, my former CFO called me from Toronto just to reminisce about old times in the compliance wars. It was remarkable to us that so many people and the media for sure seemed to view the Uber situation as a new development. The truth of the matter is that IC compliance has been a problem for a long time.

My first employment lawsuit was more than 25 years ago in 1990. (I told you it's been a problem for a long time!) An IC claimed he was our employee, because he wanted to be able to file for unemployment. ICs, by definition, are not employees, do not pay unemployment taxes, and so have no right to state unemployment compensation. They are not issued a W2 tax form for wages at the end of the year, but a 1099 form. This is why this issue is often referred to as the 1099 vs. W2 debate.

We won that case, in part because the language we used. Words matter, and the fact that in our documentation and contracts we talked about "engaging" the consultant and not "hiring" him was key. We also outlined the fact that he could engage others to do the work and was free to set his own schedule as long as the project was completed at the agreed upon time. These explicit terms established our relationship with the consultant as an independent one. Similarly, the language we had with our client was the mirror image of that with our consultants and clearly delineated the roles we would assume and specifically not assume in the process of sourcing or overseeing a project. We went on to win three subsequent cases, which on the one hand, was the desired result, but on the other was a tremendous distraction and an added cost.

By 1993, we noticed many of our technology clients becoming gun shy about the IC employee problem. Gigs that could clearly be done on an independent basis, like market research, in which the consultant would not enter the client facility until the final presentation, were canceled as the CFOs and general counsels determined that the compliance risk was too great. This risk averse market behavior presented an opportunity. As an entrepreneur, I had to figure out a way for my clients to buy the services of my consultant network, so I created a new company, Collabrus, to eliminate the IC vs. employee risk.

Like M Squared before it, Collabrus was a new work model. It acted as an employer for consultants during a project when the nature of the work or the client's risk profile warranted that the consultant be an employee. It offered specialized benefits designed for consultants, like low-cost errors and omissions insurance. In setting up and running that business, I learned more about independent contractor compliance than I ever cared to know, hence my interest in the Uber case.

With the full disclosure that I am not a lawyer, just a knowledgeable observer, I think the Uber case could go either way. One of the reasons that this is such an ambiguous area is because "independent contractor" is an undefined term in the law. Much of our employment law is derived from British master servant laws, which date back to the 14th century. In fact, they were developed following the massive carnage of the bubonic plague; because so many had died, laws were needed to define who of the remaining citizens were the masters and who were the servants. Back then, ICs were not part of the picture. So although we all know the world has changed a lot since the days of vassals and serfs, some aspects of employment law have not.

(That said, it is ironic that the word *freelancer* derives from medieval mercenary knights. Because they were not bound to any one king, they were warriors for hire. Their weapon of choice was the lance, so they were an available or a "free lance." But I digress....)

Because there is no legal definition of an IC, though some states have done so, tests have been developed that take into account agency law constructs as well as other factors. The IRS has put the most widely used framework together in its "20 Points" that define an independent contractor. These are common law tests and include things like having their own tools, being able to experience a financial loss, and receiving no training. Unfortunately, not all of the conditions need to be met, and some are more important than others. This makes for great ambiguity in who may be an IC and who may be an employee.

To try to make it simpler for employers and workers, the IRS has categorized the 20 points into three categories, behavioral control, financial control, and the relationship of the parties. In so doing, they still do not prioritize the list or suggest which are automatic determinants of an employee or contractor relationship respectively. Because clarity would be too easy, they add the following caveat, to their documentation on the subject: "The IRS emphasizes that factors in addition to the 20 factors identified in 1987 may be relevant, that the weight of the factors may vary based on the circumstances, that relevant factors may change over time, and that all facts must be examined."[1]

The following graphic illustrates the 20 points.

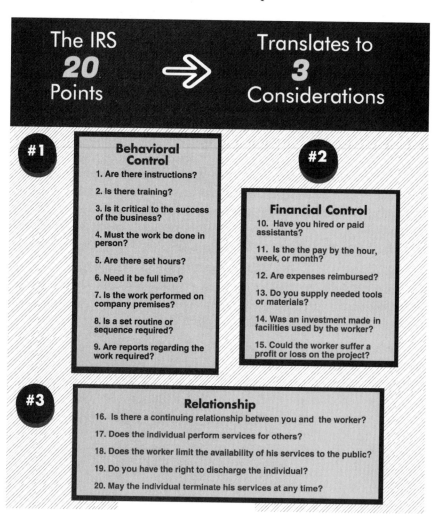

The IRS 20 Points ⟹ Translates to 3 Considerations

#1

Behavioral Control
1. Are there instructions?
2. Is there training?
3. Is it critical to the success of the business?
4. Must the work be done in person?
5. Are there set hours?
6. Need it be full time?
7. Is the work performed on company premises?
8. Is a set routine or sequence required?
9. Are reports regarding the work required?

#2

Financial Control
10. Have you hired or paid assistants?
11. Is the the pay by the hour, week, or month?
12. Are expenses reimbursed?
13. Do you supply needed tools or materials?
14. Was an investment made in facilities used by the worker?
15. Could the worker suffer a profit or loss on the project?

#3

Relationship
16. Is there a continuing relationship between you and the worker?
17. Does the individual perform services for others?
18. Does the worker limit the availability of his services to the public?
19. Do you have the right to discharge the individual?
20. May the individual terminate his services at any time?

In the last 20 years, businesses have drawn direction and control as the most important considerations from these "20 Points."

So let's consider the Uber driver. One thing Uber has going for it is that it doesn't train its drivers; drivers come to Uber knowing how to operate a vehicle. Uber may certify that the driving record be clean, but this wouldn't be considered training or direction. The fact that drivers can set their own schedule is also a plus for Uber, as it reduces that sense of control. The fact that so many drivers are very part-time (i.e., less than 10 hours), is also a plus. Technology, though, muddies the picture. Drivers are given an iPhone by Uber to be able to hook up to its ride-hailing platform. As such, Uber is providing the tools to some extent. Perhaps the biggest issue, and the one that an Administrative Law Judge highlighted in a ruling in 2015 in which he deemed a Southern California driver an employee, is that Uber sets the pricing of all rides. As such, this is preeminent control over the driver.[2]

To date, there have been three court cases, two in California and one in Florida. In each case, the driver was deemed an employee, but each case was different. As such, insights were tough to glean. By extension, the importance of these actions as precedents is difficult to discern.

If it ever does get finally adjudicated, my guess is that it could be a split decision; in some cases, of drivers who work virtually full-time for Uber and only Uber (many work for other car-hailing services like Lyft), Uber may be deemed the employer. In the case of the majority of drivers, and certainly most that I have informally polled, the incremental nature of the Uber work, which might help a teacher, house painter, or musician earn some extra money, could tip the scale to the IC side. That is what seems fair to me, some are employees and some are not. This split decision balances the need to support worker protection with the need to enable new business models that empower incremental employment and enable increased income potential for a variety of people.

Unfortunately, the picture has gotten all the more muddled. Recently in the United Kingdom, Uber drivers won the right to have vacation pay and a minimum wage. That is currently being appealed. How that settlement may or may not pertain to the U.S. case I do not know. In other developments on the U.S. case, a settlement was recently reached in the class action lawsuit meant to cover any driver who feels he or she should be an Uber employee. Uber agreed to pay $100 million to settle the matter, but the judge refused to accept the settlement, judging the dollar amount to be inadequate. On the heels of that decision was another court action that may limit the possibility of future class action lawsuits against Uber by requiring disputes to be handled through arbitration.[3] This is good news potentially for Uber, because the costs of an adverse finding could be dramatic; one estimate put the added cost, were Uber to lose the suit, at $4.1 billion.[4] It is bad news for this area of employment law, because additional clarity is needed, and this high-profile case may be the one that could finally clarify the issue.

But let's get back to the more generic situation. As an independent consultant, am I an employee or not—and why do I care?

So Why Do I Care?

Many large technology and financial services companies have become risk-averse on this employment compliance issue and have invested in talent management strategies to mitigate that risk. Some are very basic, in which a dictate has come down saying no one will be engaged to do project work on a 1099 basis. Because the company doesn't want to hire these flexible resources as employees, they require that all independent workers be paid through a third-party vendor.

Over the last 20 years, staffing companies have built "master vendor" empires in which they manage the procurement of temporary and contingent staffing for companies. Individuals who would typically be paid on a 1099 basis would be converted to a temporary staff employee in the vendor management service (VMS) world. VMS began as a way for corporations to compete more effectively by reducing procurement costs. The notion was that companies could become more efficient by reducing the numbers of vendors with whom they worked and consequently who became part of the procurement process. VMS providers would consolidate bills, manage a preferred vendor list, reduce time to fill projects, and establish set fees or pay rates for different classes of expertise. The VMS provider was compensated for its efforts with a percentage off the top of all contracting firm billings. As such, in a VMS environment the ultimate fees paid to contingent workers, whether they are junior programmers or senior communications consultants tend to be discounted to support the VMS provider.

It is unclear that the VMS model has improved corporate effectiveness. According to Aberdeen Research, an industry specialist in the field, only 17 percent of companies using a VMS system have seen spend reductions and or recruiting efficiency gains. Nonetheless, more than 72 percent of U.S. corporations use a VMS process to manage contract labor and professional services procurement.[5] Where once this was an issue affecting primarily technical resources, now it could affect any professional service supplier.

To be prepared, it is important that you know the rules. Once you know the rules, it is important to understand how they would apply to you.

To review, the three key considerations are behavioral control, financial control, and the relationship of the parties. Behavioral control is all about how the work will be done. Is training required and must it be done on site? Nowadays, site specifications are not so stringent, but there are still some high-security environments in which the expectation is that all work will be done on the premises. If your client wants to dictate working conditions, hours, locations, methodology, or required training, the gig will look like an employed situation.

Although many consultants can mitigate behavioral issues with clients, financial considerations may be tough. Most consultants set their fees by the hour. To the regulators, hourly fees are an indication of employment. I know that accountants and lawyers charge by the hour, so why can't organizational development consultants? The reason is the former group has certifications, admission to the bar or a CPA. Moreover, an hourly fee structure could also bring up wage and hour issues. We will cover those in the latter half of the chapter. Suffice it to say that although they are far more challenging to develop, project fees that are milestone driven are the most defensible fee structure when considering the employment law landscape.

Finally, the relationship with the parties is really about whether you have other clients or not. An exclusive relationship with one firm is never a good idea, if you are hoping to operate as an independent consultant. The existence of a contract explicitly defining the relationship of the worker to the client as an independent contracting arrangement would seem to be a strong indicator of the intention of the parties, but it is not a hard and fast requirement. That said, in one of my many employment actions, I was thrilled when the judge looked at the consultant who was claiming to be my employee and said, "Do you not read the contracts you sign?" The unspoken answer was probably no.

Implications for Your Business

Independent consulting practices can be operated several different ways from a business entity standpoint. Many, if not most, independent workers are sole proprietorships, just doing business as themselves. Some of those sole proprietorships will file a DBA (doing business as) statement to be able to sell services as John Smith Consulting, but will still run the income and expenses through their personal taxes. Some may opt for an S Corp, in which they have some benefit of limited liability from the corporate structure, but taxes still flow through the S Corp as personal income. Others opt for full incorporation as a C Corp, becoming employees of the corporation and enjoying many tax advantages as well as one big disadvantage: double taxation. C Corp profits are subject to income taxes, and then any income paid to the owner as dividends is also taxed.

Whatever structure you have chosen is somewhat immaterial to the employee or independent contractor issue, because the determination will come down to the specifics of any given engagement. That said, a consultant who is incorporated is far more defensible as a 1099. In fact, some companies will only consider paying a consultant on a 1099 basis if he or she is incorporated.

If you are hoping to do business as an independent contractor and are not incorporated, here are some tips to help defend your position:

- Always have more than one client. Offering service to the community at large is one of those behavioral considerations that helps define you as a business person rather than an employee.

- Similarly, having a unique business name, an investment in office space, or a unique marketing-oriented website are all signs that you are open for business to all comers.

- Also, be in control of your work circumstances. Don't let clients set hours for you. Keep in mind that you have been hired to achieve a result and how you do that is up to you and your expertise.

- Be wary of being given an entry badge that does not clearly say "visitor" on it. Similarly, avoid attending office parties that typically are for staff. As the saying goes, if it walks like a duck and talks like a duck, it must be a duck.

Conversely, some consulting engagements would be very difficult to construe as an independent situation. Long-term projects of more than six months are a case in point. Similarly, project or interim situations in which you are given hiring and firing authority could be seen as conferring responsibilities that are typically handled by employees. Finally, situations where you are doing the same work as an employee in the next office are highly suspect. Again, remember: as much as you would like to be paid as an independent on a 1099, the work will determine what is appropriate.

Any of the business structures can be paid on a 1099 basis. If you are being told that you need to be an employee, you have a few options:

- You can see if taking the step to become fully incorporated would address the issue. Be sure to consult a financial and tax advisor if considering this option.

- You can become a temporary employee of your client. Some firms are open to this option, but many are not. Some may just refer you to their master vendor firm and have you become an employee of that provider.

- You can find yourself an employer.

So I Need an Employer

In the last 10 years, a new market niche has developed in employer partners. Some came from staffing services and others from human capital companies that saw the need to empower independent contractors to work in companies concerned about the compliance issue. Companies like the one I started, Collabrus, or MBO Partners employ consultants for the duration of a gig. The client pays MBO Partners, who in turn pays you as an employee. You would receive a W2 at year end rather than a 1099. Unlike 1099 engagements, in which consulting fees are paid in full, employed consultants would receive payments net of income and employment taxes.

Most of these firms are very familiar with the now-ubiquitous master vendor service structure. As such, they have gone to great lengths to become preferred vendors under master vendor contracts at those companies who are big consumers of consultants. If you are hoping to land a contract with one of those companies with a master vendor relationship, you may want to know if the firm you opt to become employed through is already on the approved list.

In some respects, having an employer can be beneficial for a consultant. As a self-employed individual, you must pay both the entire portion of the FICA employment tax burden, or 15.3 percent. As an employee, your employer pays half of that. Additionally, you would be covered by worker's compensation insurance and unemployment insurance. Also, many of the employer partner firms offer additional benefits like access to a 401K plan, short-term disability, and/or healthcare benefits.

If you do become an employee, especially if it is not your normal mode of operation, be sure to keep in mind some additional considerations:

- When you give up your independence and become an employee, you are subject to certain rights due employees by law. For example, you must be paid no longer than 10 days after the completion of a pay period. Also be aware that employee status does not automatically confer vacation or sick pay; those benefits are voluntary not statutory.

- Understand the economics of the situation. On the one hand, you are paying less in employment taxes as an employee. In fact, many firms will try to negotiate a reduction in your fees to account for the 7.65 percent cost you do not have to bear. This may be appropriate, but also remember that your cash flow will be lower due to withholding income taxes. Alternatively, you may save money that you might spend on an accountant preparing your quarterly tax filings.

- Be attuned to policy developments on this front. One aspect of the Uber lawsuit is the attention that is being paid to this area of the law. It could be that things will change in the next five years.

A Wage and Hour Discussion

One last thing to consider if you become an employee as a consultant is the wage and hour implications. Wage and hour laws are those governed by the Fair Labor Standards Acts (FSLA). They establish the minimum wage, child protections laws, and overtime regulations.

Overtime has come under strict scrutiny in the last five years. It used to be that a job was deemed exempt or non-exempt, meaning it was exempt or not from overtime. White-collar workers and managers were considered exempt, and a non-exempt salary threshold of less that $23,666 per year sealed the deal. (The government does not like round numbers.) Most consulting engagements were more similar to management roles, so running afoul of wage and hour laws didn't seem like a problem. However, that world has changed.

Recently decisions have come down saying that retail store managers, typically considered exempt, are indeed non-exempt and should be entitled to overtime. Price Waterhouse Coopers settled a case in 2015 that sought overtime protections for junior accountants who had not yet taken the CPA exam.[6] Moreover, in 2016, the Obama administration raised the salary threshold to $47, 476 (Again, why they can't use round numbers like $47,500, I will never understand....) rendering many more types of workers potentially eligible for overtime. However, many onlookers expect the Trump administration to rescind this order.

Like the definition of employees, aside from the salary test, the definition of an exempt or non-exempt employee is murky. Considerations have to do with the nature of regular duties and their importance to the continuity of the business.

One issue that regulators pay particular attention to though is how the employee is paid. Hourly payments are, in the eyes of the government, a determination of non-exempt status. One can argue that paying a consultant $60/hour should clearly make him or her exempt, because that is about $120K per annum. However, paying that person for a three-month gig is only a W2 of $28,800. Some firms have moved to paying consultant employees a minimum exempt salary and then using additional deliverable based bonuses to account for additional fees.

That said, many consultants are horrified at the notion that the work they are doing could be considered non-exempt. As such, they would never broach the issue with their employer or client.

The bottom line is that this area of the law is messy. It could be as an employee you have the right to overtime even though you are just a consultant coming in to work on a time bounded project.

Never a dull moment in the wonderful world of employment law.

A Final Note on Employment and Digital Talent Platforms

Most of the digital talent platforms have taken a passive positon in the area of independent contractor compliance. In their contracts, they leave it to the client to decide whether or not the worker should be an employee or contractor. In some cases, this is absolutely appropriate. The programmer I finally procured from Fiverr for my website was clearly doing a short-term gig and had many other clients. However, were the platforms to develop to the point where engagements were of significant duration, the situation could be different.

More importantly, though, the platforms are often patronized by smaller firms who may be unaware of the nuances of employment law. They may engage several consultants to work alongside employees doing the same job. As Microsoft discovered back in the '90s, when it lost an enormous lawsuit because they hired contractors to do the same work as employees, this is a prescription for trouble. Many experienced and more junior managers do not appreciate the control dimension and with the good intention of getting the job right, provide a level of oversight that could be seen as instruction. That oversight, consequently, could make the project seem like employment. Similarly, some startup firms may be unaware that the talent they secured to work 60 hours a week may actually be subject to overtime even though they are consultants.

Because your clients may not be familiar with the problem, it is important that you are and that you establish the right way to be doing business. As the saying goes, "Buyer beware."

Chapter 7 Key Takeaways

- Compliance with the laws governing independent contractors and employees is a major issue in the United States.

- The IRS has 20 points that determine whether an individual is a contractor or employee, but there is no set methodology to how these rules are applied, creating significant ambiguity.

- The key factors determining an employee are behavioral control, financial control and the relationship of the parties.

- Consultants who incorporate are most immune from the W2 1099 issue.

- Consultants can be employed by firms who provide payroll services and other benefits.

- In some cases, employed consultants may be eligible for overtime, so should be aware of the rules in this area.

8

The Employee Experience as an Independent

Employee experience is one of the new terms of art in the world of work, as more and more companies are realizing that as the war for talent rages, it is important to create an employee environment in which people want to work. In fact, many of the independent workers are people who may have left the corporate world because the employee experience did not engage them. This talent drain is of concern to corporate America. Now more than ever, researchers and HR managers are investigating the employee experience to understand what makes the best work environment and what makes people want to stay in those environments. With that in mind and with full knowledge of the irony involved, I thought there could be insights from this employee experience body of knowledge to apply to independent work.

> "If you don't drive your business, you will be driven out of business."
>
> —B.C. Forbes

One of the experts in the field is Jacob Morgan, a futurist and co-founder of the Future of Work Community, a think tank of senior business leaders at global organizations, who explore how the workplace is changing and how those changes will impact people around the world. (He also produces the Future of Work podcast, which I highly recommend.) In fact, Jacob published a book on employee engagement in the spring of 2017: *The Employee Experience Advantage: How to Win the War for Talent by Giving Employees the Workspaces They Want, The Tools They Need, and a Culture They Can Celebrate.* Jacob analyzed more than 250 global organizations to determine how to create an organization where people genuinely want, not need, to show up for work. I asked Jacob if, in doing his research, he ever thought about the implications for a firm with an employee count of one. He responded, "For solo practitioners, it's quite different since these experiences are being funded by you vs. the organization. Still, the good news is that nobody knows what you care about or value most more than you!"[1]

He then went on to suggest three areas that independent workers should consider: the tools needed to get the work done, the work environment most conducive for strong performance, and company culture. So, with thanks due to Jacob, let's discuss those dimensions.

Tools of the Trade

Regardless of your specialty, there are certain "tools" an independent consultant needs to operate efficiently as an enterprise. Foremost among these are a contract framework and a financial structure. Other helpful tools are a training and development plan, a marketing plan, and a technology policy.

The Contract and Risk Framework

When an individual is hired by a company, whether as a salesperson, CFO, or receptionist, typically there is an offer letter that spells out the specifics of the arrangement. It addresses salary, benefits eligibility, work hours, start dates, and reporting relationships. Consulting engagements also need that level of detail, but keep in mind the basis of the relationship is totally different. As discussed in Chapter 7, the foundation for employment law stems from master servant relationships, where the company is the master and the employee is the servant.

Regardless of function, from web development to interim CFOs, consulting projects are conducted on a fundamentally different premise. It is a peer-to-peer interaction in which each party explicitly has something to gain as a result of the completion of the process; the client gains the results desired and the consultant earns fees. Theoretically, this same mutual aggrandizement exists in employment relationships, but there it is implicit.

Moreover, in a contractual situation, if the desired result is not achieved, the payment need not be made. This is because the legal foundation is in contract law, not employment law. That is why contracts are critical in defining the implications of performance or non-performance in a consulting agreement. For those that may have a hard time getting your heads around the notion, I liken it to hiring a contractor to paint every room in your house. If they do not paint the kitchen, you can withhold payment. If they do a terrible job painting the kitchen (e.g., they only do three walls), you can withhold payment, because the contracted result was not delivered. Consulting contracts are much the same.

That said, a contract for an independent worker need not be long and complicated; depending on your particular area of expertise, it could be quite simple. You could use a letter format that includes the key provisions essential to your business. Alternatively, you may often be signing the contract of your client. In that case, you want to know which clauses you will accept, which you may want to negotiate, and which you may want to add. Don't try to add all of your points, just the most important ones. You do need to be sure that you understand the implications of the additional points a client may insert. There could be some risks you are willing to assume and others you can mitigate with insurance coverages, a subject I will address at the end of this section. Finally, you may have a high-risk tolerance and decide that given your clientele, you are comfortable with any exposure. That is why I called this tool a contract framework; the key is to identify the risk dimensions inherent in your work, and determine which ones you can live with and which you can't. Understanding the risk exposures will help you construct a set of letters, contracts, and/ or insurance coverages that affords you the right level of protection.

That said, this section may be moot, if you opt to work for a third-party employer such as MBO Partners. In that case, many of these issues will be addressed for you. I will cover that option at the end of this section.

Typical Provisions

Here are the things you want to be sure to think about as you develop your contract framework.

Agreement on the Scope of Work

It is critical that you and your client are in full agreement about what the project will and will not include. At the most basic level, if a recommendation is to be made, be sure to agree on the form that it will take. A client who is expecting a 30-page report may feel that the result was not achieved if the end product is a 10-slide deck. There should also be explicit agreement on:

- Resources the client has agreed to dedicate to the project.
- Timelines.
- Interim reports and deliverables.
- Acceptance of the final project.

Fees and Payment Terms

Once you have determined the project price, the key contractual issue is timing. If payments are late, will you charge a late fee? Will there be a grace period? For projects done on a percent of completion basis, you will need to define how compensable percentages will be determined.

Reimbursable expenses should also be explicitly understood. This is especially important for a consultant who may need to travel long distance for a project. If you are regularly spending five hours on an airplane, will that time be reimbursed? A good rule of thumb is to be reimbursed for at least 50 percent of the time, especially if you can work on the plane. Similarly, regarding hotel expenses, it should be clear the type of costs that will be covered and the price points that are acceptable to the client; a Courtyard Marriott may fit the bill, whereas the Four Seasons would not. At M Squared, we did several projects in South Africa that were well more than nine months in duration, so even more travel negotiations were required. In addition to the standard travel and lodging details, we also negotiated a set number of trips back to the United States during the course of the engagement. Providing as much information about anticipated expenses before the project begins is a good way to reduce the risk that your client may dispute these costs.

Relationship of the Parties

If you are assuming a project as an independent contractor, then you should say so in your agreement. Despite the discussion in the last chapter about how murky independent contractor compliance is, spelling out your intention to be an independent does not hurt. You should state affirmatively that as an independent contractor you understand you are not entitled to unemployment, workers' compensation, or any other benefits typically offered to employees. You may also need to state that you have reviewed the necessary insurance coverages and opted to secure or not secure the requisite plans. I will discuss insurance a bit more at the end of this section.

Additional Contractual Issues

The issues previously mentioned can easily be addressed in an engagement letter, preferably one that is signed and/or acknowledged by both parties. For multi-page documents, blocks for initials on every page can be a god idea.

Consultants working at the most senior levels often require more detailed provisions. The following items are typically found in contracts, but could be addressed in a more informal document like an engagement letter as well.

Intellectual Property

Intellectual property (IP) is becoming more and more important in consulting contracts. As an employee, your work product belongs to your employer on the basis of the "work for hire" body of law. As an independent worker, your work product is your own unless it is stipulated otherwise.

Many clients will ask consultants to waive their IP rights. This can be done simply by describing the project as work for hire. Alternatively, you can specifically state that you assign all ownership rights to your client. Similarly, you could offer a license, which could be at a fee or gratis, for perpetual use, so that the client can share in the invention.

There are clients who are even stricter in their interpretation of IP laws. Some companies, especially in the entertainment industry insert a *droit morale* clause, which requires the contractor to cede not only ownership rights but moral rights to an idea as well. This was an issue for my firm when we did some work with Disney. I remember being a bit appalled at the idea of waiving moral rights. (That said, there are many things in the law which I find appalling, including the independent contractor definition.) My lawyer explained it to me as follows: If a consultant decides it would be great idea to put a moustache on Mickey Mouse, that could turn out to be a wildly popular idea that could have attendant increases in revenue from the merchandising of that idea. But because Disney owns Mickey, Disney has the right to any representation of the character regardless of who came up with the idea of said moustache. Hence, they ask vendors to waive their moral rights. If you are in the idea side of a business, then you may encounter this issue. In which event, be sure to consult your attorney so you can understand the implications of the *droit morale* clause.

Non-Disclosure Agreements

A corollary to IP provisions is the non-disclosure agreement, commonly referred to by its acronym, the NDA. Many technology companies require NDAs from any management-level employee or contractor. I needed to sign an NDA just to enter LinkedIn headquarters when I was researching this book.

An NDA requires the signer not divulge any proprietary information, trade secrets, or patents to anyone outside the company. Many people disregard NDAs, as they feel they are unenforceable, especially in California. That may be true sometimes, but a well-crafted NDA can be powerful protection. If your client can prove that you intentionally violated the agreement, they may be entitled to injunctive relief, damages, and even compensation for lost profit.

Your exposure in signing an NDA is limited to your understanding of what material is protected under the agreement, so be sure you understand what is considered proprietary so that you do not accidentally violate any provision. Frequently, for example, client lists are considered trade secrets. For those well versed in a particular industry, knowledge that may be covered by the agreement could be knowledge you acquired from elsewhere. In this case, you should work with your client to narrow the scope of the agreement or add some carve outs of items not covered to ensure there is no unintended breach.

Indemnifications and Disputes

Many consultants include indemnifications to protect against the horror of abject failure. The best indemnifications are ones that are mutual. Your client holds you harmless in certain situations and you do the same. Such provisions are best drafted with legal assistance or at least reviewed by an attorney well versed in contracts.

A related provision would be how to handle disputes. Because everyone wants to avoid litigation, the typical courses are arbitration and mediation. In either case, and this is especially true if you are signing a client contract, make sure there is "limited discovery." Discovery is the time-consuming and expensive part of the legal process, which involves collecting data about the dispute. This could be in the form of interviews or depositions, which are very expensive because the attorneys of both parties need to be present. Asking for arbitration in lieu of litigation does not limit your financial exposure, if the discovery is unlimited. Again, when in doubt, consult a lawyer first, so that you will not have to consult them later.

Mediation is another dispute resolution option. As I used to tell my HR students, mediation is, at its core, throwing money at the problem. It is a way to meet a financial settlement by using a trained mediator. The rules of evidence and the facts about who may be in the right do not necessarily have the import they would in an arbitration or in litigation. It is not my favorite dispute resolution technique, but it is probably the least costly, especially for an independent worker.

Keep in mind, as my attorney once said to me, a contract is a living document. As you negotiate different points with clients, you may find loopholes or provisions that need to be reconsidered. It is good practice to revise your contract once every few years.

The Freelancer's Union has a contract creator tool that enables individuals to design custom contracts. Not unsurprisingly, the tool was built by freelance programmers and vetted for accuracy by freelance attorneys.

Insurance Coverages

The key to negotiating any contract is understanding the risks that are being mitigated by the tool and calibrating those against your own risk management tolerance. That said, some risks can be handled by insurance. You may not need an indemnification provision, for example, if you have Errors and Omissions (E&O) insurance for your practice. E&O insurance, also called professional liability insurance, is for consultants what medical malpractice is for doctors; neither intends to make a mistake, but in the event an unfortunate incident occurs, insurance will cover the liability. E&O typically comes in two flavors: claims made or per occurrence. The former is cheaper, but must be in place before the event that triggers the claim occurs. Occurrence-based E&O is more comprehensive and more expensive. Some consultants may opt to purchase this selectively in the case of high impact projects where even a low probability claim would have a significantly negative financial consequence.

Certain client companies require any vendor, whether independent or not, to carry certain insurance coverages, including E&O. On projects for which a car will be used, they often require auto coverage, which can be easily added to your existing personal auto policy. Be sure to add the additional premium cost into your business expenses.

The tricky one is workers' compensation insurance, which protects against injuries in the workplace. If you are injured on site because you helped move a printer from point A to point B, that would be a workers' comp claim. More importantly, though, if you got carpal tunnel in your home office by working on a client project, you could still have a workers' comp claim against your client. That is why many companies prefer that a consultant be covered by his or her own workers' comp provider, so that any claims that could arise would not inure to the firm policy.

However, as a company of one, you are not required to carry workers' comp; most states will allow you to exclude yourself from mandatory workers' compensation programs. As such, it can be a conundrum.

One solution to that issue is to engage a professional partner to handle your employment and contractual issues. MBO Partners and others, like TalentWave, provide an array of services for consultants. (We will talk more about this option in Chapter 9.) For a client that will not relent on the workers' comp front, a consulting employment platform may be the best option.

Financial Structure

Regardless of your functional specialty, you need to be able to manage the financial end of your practice. At the very basic level, you need to bill clients, collect monies, and pay expenses. For most consultants, except perhaps the accountants, this is one of the least favorite aspects of running a business, but that is changing as more and more products are being released in the cloud targeting small businesses. These products allow you to set up a basic accounting system to be able to track income and expenses as well as calculate your profit, loss, and estimated taxes. Of course, once you set up your business financial system, it is always a good idea to review it with your tax advisor or accountant.

Perhaps the largest player in the small business accounting world is QuickBooks. It now has a version for the independent work world called QuickBooks Self-Employed. It has features that will review (with permission) the transactions in your bank account to help identify those that are likely to be business-related expenses. Similarly, FreeAgent.com is a product developed for this marketplace. In addition to the invoicing and reporting, it also includes a project estimating tool, a time tracking feature, and the ability to use a smartphone to upload and track expenses. FreeAgent.com is a British company but it does have a U.S. version.

In addition to these two, there are a host of products that would work for small businesses and independent professionals like FreshBooks, Wave, and LessAccounting. One web-based product, Xero, integrates with Timesheets.com, a time and billing system for companies that is always free for freelancers. (I provide an overview of many apps targeted at freelancers in Chapter 9.)

If the idea of managing your own accounting system seems daunting, there are other options. You can hire a firm or individual to do it for you. Peers.org is a marketplace for independents that would provide a place to start looking for those resources.

Alternatively, you can look to the employment platform world of firms such as MBO Partners or TalentWave. These firms will not provide you with a business P&L, rather you will become their employee. They will handle all invoicing, time management, and collections. They also offer expense reporting options. Additionally, they provide benefits including health insurance, workers' comp coverage, E&O insurance, and retirement programs.

As discussed in the previous section, if you do opt to run your own business, you will need to secure insurance. At the very least, E&O and medical insurance. If you operate out of a physical space that is not your residence, you may need general liability coverage as well. Some coworking spaces may require a certificate of insurance, so be sure to check the fine print on those agreements.

Other Key Tools

To maintain your professional edge as a consultant, whether you are a blogger or a CFO, you will need to spend some time investing in yourself. Like any business, you should set up your own training and development plan. What skills do you need to bolster to get more business? Are there seminars or trade shows that you should be attending? For some professions, such as human resources, there could be required or recommended continuing education programs put on by major industry associations. Many individuals consider these programs as they come up, rather than taking a long view. It is best to think of these opportunities to build your intellectual capital and marketability in the aggregate to get a more strategic view and to better understand which programs, at what cost, would have the best return to your business.

This is true of your marketing approach as well. Are there events you should be attending that would be great networking opportunities from a business development perspective? Factor those into your budgeting. Do not forget to include networking events, marketing materials, website hosting, graphic design services, and association membership fees.

A technology policy is another good idea in today's world where you can sign up for subscriptions and forget that you have them. Of course you have your computer, phone, and printer expenses, but what other services do you intend to purchase? Might you need a Survey Monkey subscription to conduct your research, or a Pictograph one to add infographics to your blog? Conversely, if you need one of these, can you charge it to a client, or is it an ongoing cost to your business? (This is one of those questions you may want to discuss with your financial advisor as well.) Do you have the LinkedIn Pro package or the regular free setting? Are you hiring web developers from Fiverr to keep your site up to date? You should consider all of these technology expenses to understand their cost in your business.

Your Work Environment

Physical work spaces are one of the key elements of an employee engagement strategy. As such, it should be part of yours as well for your single employee enterprise.

It is no surprise that the coworking marketplace has grown tremendously just as the gig market has, since the two are directly correlated. In 2007 there were 75 coworking spaces worldwide, and by 2015 there were 7,800.[2] The increase in the number of skilled independents is driving this shared office space explosion.

WeWork, the largest of the new coworking providers, has a market cap of $10 billion, is the fourth-largest real estate firm in the country and is the poster child for the power of the Gig Economy. Real estate industry analysts acknowledge that the long-time coworking firm Regus went into bankruptcy following the tech crash of 2001, when it lost its short-term customers and could no longer fund its long-term leases. WeWork operates under a similar economic model, but now, independent workers comprise a significant portion of its business. Previously, the short-term rental space was let to sales offices or startups, all of which would be vulnerable in an economic contraction. The rise of alternative workers as a market segment and WeWork's cultivation and understanding of gig and sharing economy needs makes their model more resilient in times of economic uncertainty. Its market success has inspired many others to join the fray. Coworking spaces such as Spaces, Bespoke CoWorking, and PivotDesk can offer desks by the week or month to enable more of an office feel for those who need it. In Mill Valley, a suburb of San Francisco, the Hivery is a coworking space aimed at women. It markets itself as a place where women can create, collaborate, and support each other, appealing to entrepreneurs, moms returning to work, and retired Baby Boomers.

However, be sure to check out the various options in person to see what suits you best. One of the interviews I had for this book was at a WeWork space in San Francisco. It was a Friday afternoon, and we were seated near a ping-pong table. The atmosphere was hip, noisy, and somewhat distracting, as ping-pong balls flew wildly through the air and almost hit me several times. This work environment might not fly for everyone, pardon the pun. Similarly, Regus, which has emerged from bankruptcy and still operates in most markets, is much more corporate and may be too staid and stultifying for some.

A key consideration for coworking space is the expense. Following is a comparison of several different San Francisco spaces in what is a hip neighborhood, the South of Market or SOMA area. Most providers offer single-day charges as well as meeting room fees. Regus requires a 24-month agreement. Be sure to check out the fine print to understand all expenses if you enter such an arrangement.

Co-Working Space Monthly Fees

	Any Desk	Dedicated Desk	Office
Citizen Space*	$200	$425	Not Quoted
Parisoma*	$345	$595	$1250
Regus**	Not Quoted	$342	$798
Space Works*	$340	$510	$780
WeWork*	$220	$350	$400

Based on website rates for San Francisco South of Market accessed on 12/31/2016

**Based on lowest South of Market location for one person for 30 days from proposal emailed by Regus 12/31/2016*

The design thinking today, which is clearly adhered to in coworking facilities, is to incorporate a range of options into work spaces to enable employees to perform optimally. There should be a well-designed ergonomic space for focus work, when you need to concentrate and dig deep into a subject. Most people prefer this to be a private space, separate from others to limit distractions. Architects and designers today incorporate comfortable spaces as well for congregating during the day, but often as another choice for reading and/or working on a laptop away from the desk. Lighting is key and needs to be sufficiently bright in task-specific areas. Sound baffling can also be critical in spaces that support different activities. Storage and access to key materials also makes for more efficiency.

Leisure space is an important consideration. Most facilities incorporate a kitchen as well as informal couch seating. Some have distinct play areas, sporting anything from foosball tables to ping-pong to pinball games.

According to a recent *Harvard Business Review* piece, another key aspect of a work environment that can enhance engagement is color. Those involved in mental work should be relaxed when working. A relaxed environment would be one that is somewhat bright and uncluttered, with limited visual complexity. Stark modernism is not conducive, by the way, despite that fact that many coworking facilities tend toward that aesthetic.[3]

If your work environment is in your home, you should incorporate these ideas as you plan your workspace or reconfigure an existing space. Make sure your workspace has not just a desk, but potentially an easy chair or sofa as well. Maybe you can't repaint to a relaxing color, but decluttering a space could help. Understand what level of noise works for you; some people need a constant hum with music, while others prefer silence. Privacy is a related factor. Do you want to be working in a space where you are in the middle of a lively home environment, or do you crave seclusion when hard at work?

Another issue is how often as a solo practitioner you may need to meet with other people. If you are likely to have collaborators, where will in-person meetings be convened? Like many entrepreneurs, I started my company, M Squared, in an upstairs bedroom. (I actually had to shut the door as a symbolic way to demonstrate to myself that I was at work.) As I began having more and more meetings with clients and consultants, coffee, lunch and parking bills began to add up, prompting us to lease office space. That was 25 years ago. In today's world, the ability to secure conference rooms through sharing economy companies such as Liquid Space makes the decision to lease traditional office space or even coworking space a bit different. If one only require a conference room a few times a month, $75 per use may make more sense than leasing office space or a coworking slot for four times that amount.

Ultimately, you need to consider all of the various options and determine what office situation works for you. Then you can create the best environment for you to thrive.

Company Culture

For so many consultants, becoming independent is a lifestyle choice; becoming an independent was motivated in part by the desire to take control over life and build a rewarding and flexible career. By definition, that has cultural implications. Although you may work very hard at your client projects, you probably want to play hard, too, or at least work on your own terms. That ethos of why you work as you do is part of the company culture of your company of one.

A big idea in employee engagement today is the notion of "moments that matter." Companies of all sorts are trying to celebrate key moments with employees, whether it be a family event, such as the birth of a child; a life milestone, such as buying a house; or a career event, such as a major promotion. You may want to think of your solo enterprise in that context. What are the moments that will matter to you?

It could be that you want to celebrate the growth of your business. When I was in YEO (the Young Entrepreneur's Organization), one of my fellow entrepreneurs would buy herself a piece of jewelry whenever she hit a major revenue milestone. (The gem when she went from $3 million to $5 million was lovely.) There is no reason why you can't make similar symbolic acknowledgments of your progress as you meet milestones, whether it's revenues, number of clients, or number of years in business.

The key aspect here is the idea of celebrating your successes as a company. This would be part of your culture. Even a one-person company can have a culture. Will yours be formal (e.g., nine-to-five) or more free-form depending on the day? In your branding exercise, you defined your core values. If one of them involves community service, how will that play into your culture? Will you give a portion of your profits to charity, or perhaps donate your time and expertise to the community?

Conversely, do you need to take steps to ensure that because you are in control of your time, you do not spend all of your time working? There are definitely times when you need to put your head down and just keep working on a project until it is completed. (Writing a book is like that, by the way.) But working 16 hours a day should not be a steady state schedule for most people. For your own mental health, you should build time into your schedule that allows you to have downtime to work out, catch up with friends, or play golf. If your schedule says that from 7 until 9 a.m. you are at the gym, perhaps you won't schedule your client meeting until 10. Sometimes you may need to reschedule the gym, but many times you won't.

Being explicit about your intentions about time, whether it is your personal time or that you give to the community, will add heft to your business. Even though that heft may be intangible, there will be more for you to stand behind. Moreover, when you bring other independent workers into your company to assist with a big project, you will have more to say about your business. It isn't just me, a computer, and a phone; I am creating a work environment that enables me to excel at my craft, bring value to clients, and potentially serve my community.

Even a company of one has a culture.

Chapter 8 Key Takeaways

- To create the optimal employee experience for yourself you need the right tools, work environment, and culture.

- Understanding what aspects of typical contract provisions are important to your business is the first step in building a contracting framework that you can apply flexibly to your business.

- Consultants need a financial structure that will enable them to run the business effectively.

- Corporate platforms that provide payroll services to consultants can assume some of the burden of running a business for those who would like to simplify the operation.

- You need to create the office environment that will provide the workspace to enable you to do your best work.

- You can rent slices of office space to meet your needs through coworking options.

- Consider what elements you want to add to your own corporate culture to keep the business vigorous and meaningful for you.

9

The Gig Economy Ecosystem

As an independent consultant and business owner, you are on your own. As I mentioned in Chapter 4, you are an island. That said, you are not an uncharted one. Like the Greek Islands filled with yachts, fishing boats, private planes, and hydrofoils, there is an ecosystem designed to bring provisions, visitors, news and support of all kinds to your island. The players are different, from sailboats to "puddle jumper" aircraft. You need to understand the nuances, determine which is right for you, and make the most of the eco system.

"We are all in this together by ourselves."

—Lily Tomlin

Many dimensions of running your business can be outsourced to companies or individuals. Similarly, there are firms, software packages, websites, and technology platforms designed to make your life easier as an independent professional. To clarify, I am not including the digital talent platforms through which you might procure business in this set of services. Let's start at the top with the employment services platforms.

Employment Platforms

If you don't want to go through the hassle of running your own business, working through an employment platform makes sense. That said, there are significant differences to understand, not the least of which is the orientation and heritage of the provider.

There are many players in the business, from MBO Partners to Work Market to ZeroChaos. Many, if not most, are dedicated to solving the independent contractor compliance problem for their clients. They want to ensure that those employment risks we discussed in Chapter 7 don't create headaches or penalties for clients. Some are very focused on the client companies and not so much on the worker. They offer independent compliance assessments as well as criminal background verifications, sanction and/or watch list reviews, drug tests, and credit checks. They identify themselves as Employer of Record (EOR) firms, positioned to assume employer responsibility for workers a client would prefer not to hire, whether for budgetary reasons, headcount constraints, and/or administrative headaches.

If you do have a choice and/or if you are taking the initiative on your own to find an employment partner, look for those companies that also offer solutions for consultants. MBO Partners is one of the leaders in this space, in part, because they were built with the worker in mind. In fact, "MBO" stands for their original name, which was "My Business Office." They were founded in the early days of the Internet, when it appeared new technologies could cause a major disruption in the labor market. Unlike other players, at that time, MBO Partners appealed to the workers who wanted to set up an effective independent option online.

Today MBO offers a comprehensive suite of services designed for independent workers. You can select the system that best works for you, including one to optimize your business if you decide to incorporate. MBO is so expert in the market, they can deliver the services that work for the sole proprietor as well as the ones that are tailored for a professional corporation. Other services include:

- Acting as the Employer of Record.
- Up to $10 million in liability insurance.
- Contract review and administration services.
- Automated invoicing of your time and hours to your clients.
- Automated payroll with direct deposit and appropriate tax withholdings.
- Expense compliance review and processing.
- Quarterly tax administration for 1099s or corporate receipts.
- Tax-advantaged vehicles, including solo 401K.

As an aside, the new PWC digital talent platform uses MBO Partners to qualify the employment status of independent workers who apply to be members. The application incorporates a survey probing the nature of an individual's consulting practice. Following the survey, the applicant is told on what basis he or she should work.

Talent Wave is another player in this space. Although targeted more at client companies, it does offer specialized services to consultants including assistance with the preparation of Statement of Work Projects, pre-qualifying those who want to work as 1099s with the client, providing access to healthcare benefits, speedy payment, and contract management.

Finally, Collabrus is a firm I founded more than 20 years ago to manage contractor compliance. Because we started the firm to enable the senior consultants at M Squared to have an employer, we had the needs of that demographic in mind. It offers targeted benefits including access to a group health plan, a 401K plan with a match, low cost E&O insurance, commuter benefits, and a Section 125 plan to enable pretax deductions of certain medical and childcare expenses.

This list is not exhaustive. The message is that if you need an employment platform there are several good options from which to choose.

Access to Benefits and Services

If you decide to go it on your own, there is no need to re-create the wheel. There are many sites that can help you get the assistance you need to secure a wide variety of benefits. Here are a few:

Freelancers Union: Freelancers Union is one of the first organizations established to support independent workers and advocate for them in the policy community. The Freelancers Union website says, "We give independent workers a powerful voice through political action, research, and thought leadership. We aim to ensure that independent contractors receive adequate rights, protections and professional benefits."[1] Benefits offered include:

- Access to health, dental, and vision programs.
- Retirement benefits including a 401K sweep program.
- Discounts for various businesses service often needed by independents, such as accounting firms, Geico insurance, Squarespace website hosting, and Zipcar.
- Assistance with client non-payment.

The Freelancers Union also has the custom contracting tool, which I mentioned in Chapter 8.

Also worth mentioning is the organization's assistance with delinquent client payments. For years, it has offered a client score-card to allow members to rate its clients, especially in the area of timely payment. Client non-payment can be a big issue for many free agents. New York city, in fact, recently passed a law, the Freelance Isn't Free Act, that requires that freelancers be paid either by the contract date terms or 30 days after the completion of the work. It also prohibits the practice of offering a lesser fee for speedy payment.[2]

Peers.org: Peers is another not-for-profit advocacy organization that offers access to resources needed by the independent worker. Its mission is to help those in the sharing economy, and it offers special services for those providers, such as management services for AirBnB listings, remote key exchange services for home- or car-sharing, and concierge services for home-sharing hosts. It also offers services applicable to those in the gig world including:

- Health insurance, including dental and vision.
- Life insurance, including disability.
- Retirement savings programs.

Peers also is an aggregator of sharing and Gig Economy sites. Through Peers, you can access all of the various talent platforms arranged by ride-sharing, house services, home stays, skills and talents, teaching, care giving, errands and cleaning, and professional/freelance.

Stride Health: Stride Health is a San Francisco–based insurance information platform that went live in 2014. It is designed to be a recommendation engine for independent workers who are searching appropriate coverage for both themselves and their families. It has partnered with various on-demand marketplaces, including Uber, Postmates, and TaskRabbit, to ensure it reaches independent workers. It uses its own algorithms to predict the health costs of clients and then shops the web to find the best price and feature match. A search, it touts, can take just 10 minutes.

Alliance Direct Benefits: Alliance Direct Benefits is a not-for-profit organization dedicated to providing advocacy, education, and health benefits to small businesses and their families. It has been around for 40 years, and now its target also includes freelancers and the self-employed. It is not an insurer; rather it is a membership organization that, due to scale, can get buying power leverage. In other words, as an individual, you have access to group rate plans for medical benefits, travel discounts, or legal services.

Bunker Insurance: Bunker Insurance is a platform for Errors and Omissions insurance coverage (the purpose of which we discussed in Chapter 8). It is designed for freelancers who are required to have certain insurance coverages by their clients. Conversely, it also works on the client side to manage the necessary compliance tracking. It was started by Chad Nitschke, a 15-year insurance veteran, who saw that the traditional insurance market was not structured to enable independent consultants and/or their clients to secure quickly and efficiently the insurance coverages required for consulting contracts. The Bunker platform was designed to create a marketplace for contract-related insurance that would eliminate this problem for these independent workers and their clients.

Honest Dollar: Honest Dollar provides retirement vehicles for independent workers including IRAs, Roth IRAs, and SEP IRAs. It even has a retirement app to make it easy to keep your accounts funded. It has had a special affinity with independent workers and created at one point a retirement product for payroll clients who wanted to offer retirement vehicles to the independent workers they deployed; these clients would pay their independent workers via the Honest Dollar system and it would enable the independent workers to direct a portion of the fee payments into specific retirement vehicles. Just as Honest Dollar was getting media attention for this in spring 2016, Goldman Sachs purchased the Texas-based company.

Ubiquity: Ubiquity is a San Francisco–based "fin tech" firm that is focused on providing retirement vehicles for small business and sole proprietorships, or as its website says, the "other 40 million."[3] The company has its own version of an individual 401K, which it calls a "single(k)." It has a flat fee and can be set up online. A single(k) enables an independent to make a larger contribution to retirement then would be allowed in a typical IRA or Roth IRA.

Business Services and Apps

There are also many tools and services designed to make your life as an independent easier. In researching this book, I conducted a survey of independent consultants via Survey Monkey. I wanted to understand their perceptions of the pros and cons of running a business as an independent worker. I had just less than 100 respondents, so not an enormous sample, but enough to get a sense of their leanings. Not unsurprisingly, the thing they loved most about their "job" was the client work. Similarly, creating thought leadership pieces was also highly rated. The things they didn't like were accounting and collections, marketing, and, of course, sales.

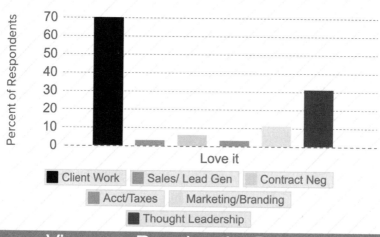

As discussed in Chapter 8, there are many tools and services to handle your accounting issues. There are also services that will help you with some of the other areas, including contract management, productivity, communication, and social media. There is even a freelancer-oriented sales management system that helps you track leads, pending deals, and closed deals. Given the world of continuous innovation and apps for everything, I cannot offer a comprehensive list, but the following offers those that have received the most buzz and/or positive reviews.

Tools for Independent Workers

Getting the Gig

Sales Management	Insightly	Capsule CRM	Streak	ContactMe	Desktime	Funnel
Proposals	Proposify	BidSketch				
Social Media	HootSuite	Buffer	TweetDeck	Tweriod	Buffer App	

Working the Gig

Project Management	Asana	Podio	Trello	Wrike	Freedcamp	Vorex	
Time Tracking	Timely	Harvest	Toggl	Freelancy	HubStaff	Cushion	Timesheets.com
Productivity	Teux Deux	Wunderlist	NowDoThis	Helium	FocusBooster		

Getting Paid

Accounting	Fresh Books	QuickBooks	Wave	Zoho	Paymo
Expense Mgt.	Shoeboxed	Expensify	Xpenditure		
Contracts/Legal	Bonsai	Shake	W9 Platform		

The Community

There are many ways to create a sense of community in your independent work lifestyle. As I said in my last book, it is not a coincidence that the rise of independent consulting as a profession coincided with the phenomenal growth of Starbucks. For many it became an alternative to the corporate water cooler—a place to mingle with others, to meet colleagues, to have team meetings. Anyone who has ever wandered into a Starbucks or another coffee house at 2 p.m. and wondered, "Who are all these people with computers sitting around?" The answer is that a good many of them are potentially gig workers.

Professional associations and civic organizations can provide a sense of community in your functional or industry profession. Coworking spaces also provide some level of affiliation. At WeWork, for example, office renters are called members, and there are many member events, including a summer camp. The Hivery, a coworking space in Mill Valley, California, a suburb of San Francisco, is a specialized networking space just for women. It offers all sorts of events to members, such as writer's workshops, entrepreneur circles, and meditation Mondays, all intended to build a sense of community.[4] Again, if the cost of that work space option works for you, the community atmosphere may make afford additional benefits for you.

Finally, there are several websites and blogs that are targeted at the freelancing and/or independent work community. They provide articles of interest on topics that affect the independent worker, such as how to manage a delinquent client, finding clients in unusual ways, and the best coffee shops in which to do business.

The digital talent platform Upwork has a link to the top 100 websites for freelancers. Because that is a bit much to digest, Upwork breaks it down by top sites overall, then it further segments it by the best for graphic designers, illustrators and animators, software developers, freelance web designers, bloggers, freelance writers, copywriting and marketing, social media, and special purpose blogs.[5] Choose the ones that seem helpful to you to pick up tips on how to better manage your business.

Chapter 9 Key Takeaways

- Employment platforms provide services like invoicing, collections, and tax withholding, allowing you to simplify the business of running your practice.

- There are several entities that can provide independent contractors deals on health benefits, retirement programs, and/or liability insurance.

- There are many tools targeted at the freelance marketplace to help make everything from accounting to marketing to time management a bit easier.

- Coworking space can offer community of many sorts if you can afford the tariff.

10

The Future of the Gig Economy, Part 1: Policy and Politics

The many reports on the Gig Economy may have different definitions of participation and different estimates of size, but they all share one thing: They see the trend of independent work continuing to grow worldwide. The McKinsey Global Institute (MGI) study suggested 18 percent annual growth for the independent workforce in the future. MGI attributes this growth in part to the increase in venture capital funding for digital talent platforms from $57 million in 2010 to more than $4 billion in 2014.[1] The MBO Partners study expects that the number of independent workers in the United States will grow 16.4 percent and comprise 41 percent of the non-farm workforce by 2021.[2] The international staffing giant Randstad goes even further, suggesting that by 2025, more than 50 percent of the workforce will be alternative workers, or, in its parlance, agile workers.[3]

"Prediction is very difficult, especially if it is about the future."

—Niels Bohr

This growth is a global phenomenon. One of the key findings in the MGI study was the extent of the growth in alternative work arrangements worldwide. Not only in the United States, but in most European countries, at least a quarter of the population participates in some way in alternative work structures, a participation rate that was much higher than the study's authors expected.[4]

Independent Work Is a Global Force

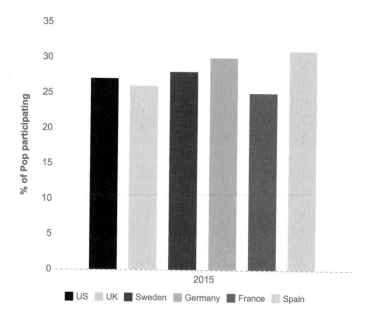

The Global Independent Workforce

■ US　░ UK　■ Sweden　■ Germany　■ France　░ Spain

Similarly, there are an array of digital platforms serving all levels of the expertise pyramid, from ride-hailing services such as Didi in China to consulting platform Expert 360 in Australia. Moreover, many U.S. platforms, such as Fiverr, have a global network of workers. Indeed, it is difficult for many junior programmers in the United States to get gigs on Fiverr, because they compete with very-low-cost competitors from the developing world, who bid projects at very low rates.

This worldwide growth is predicated on a number of factors, including technology, demographic trends, and worker empowerment. Technology inexorably reshapes our lives. In the last 20 years, we have seen the exponential growth of the Internet, social media, and mobile communications.

But it is the advent of the cloud, according to Stephen DeWitt, the CEO of the workforce automation software company WorkMarket, that is accelerating the changes in the workplace. Processing power is no longer constrained, as another server can be added in the cloud. Algorithms can therefore be developed to identify matches for any number of parametric problems, from genome sequences to specialized talents. For many of us in the Boomer generation, this is hard to fathom. As I write this as a citizen of the digital world who started my career in the analog one, I still remember the pink "while you were out" phone slips, dumb terminals, and Netscape. But Gen Xers and Millennials do not have those work experiences. For those worker cohorts, technological developments are a fact of life and the acceptance of the new approaches that result are far more readily and quickly adopted. In fact, starting in the 1990s, extensive change management programs designed to help workers, mostly Boomers, adapt to new technologies were big business for many consulting firms. Now in firms with large Millennial populations, change management has been displaced by a four-hour training session. Innovation in the cloud is now plug and play.

Meanwhile the composition of the workforce is changing as well, forcing companies to consider many different types of workers. Ten thousand Boomers retire every day, a fact that impacts certain industries more than others.[5] Wayne Cascio, the Robert Reynolds Chair of Global Leadership at The University of Colorado and a former chair of the Society for Human Resource Management (SHRM), notes that many utilities are disproportionately impacted in their linesmen operations, which could mean that downed power lines after storms may take longer to repair as the new crop of workers are not as experienced as their retired predecessors. As such, companies will need to source new workers in the traditional marketplace as well as the alternative, independent marketplace.

With the growing adoption of independent work has also come the empowerment of workers to have more control over their working lives. Various industry studies, from the MGI study to the Randstad report, have noted that flexibility and control are key factors in the increased desirability of project-based work. The government is noticing this, too. In a recent speech, Federal Reserve Governor Lael Brainard noted that the desire for flexibility is a key accelerator of the growth in the Gig Economy.[6] The new work modes and their associated technologies are making it easier for individuals to work their desired hours per week. This could be a decrease in hours, for those who can afford it, an increase for those who want to work more than the standard 40-hour week or an inconstant number, for those who prefer a totally variable pattern of work activity.

This growth will have implications across our economy. The legal and regulatory framework around employment law is poised to change. The issue of the social safety net for independent workers is one that will need to be addressed as well. Companies will need to organize differently to get the most out of the independent workforce, which suggests some attendant changes to our education system. Finally, individuals will need to understand all of these developments to maneuver in the new world. More importantly, though, they also need to manage their careers differently to succeed in this evolving marketplace. It's a tall order to look into the future, so I will start with the policy implications in this chapter. (Chapter 11 will address how businesses and independent workers we can prepare to thrive in the Gig Economy.)

That said, I do want to offer a disclaimer. Many portions of this book have been difficult to write, because new studies are coming out about the Gig Economy constantly. Several of the reports I have referenced throughout were published as I was writing the book. Suffice it to say, it is difficult to be comprehensive and accurate when describing a moving target. Nowhere is that truer than in this chapter about the future and how governmental policies may or may not reframe certain dimensions of the issue. Not only do we have the normal uncertainty associated with predictions, but we have the very roiled environment following the unexpected result of the 2016 U.S. presidential election. I will include a sidebar on pages 166–167 about what various experts are suggesting may occur in the talent marketplace under a Trump administration. For those who may read this years later, please consider it an interesting historical (or hysterical) anecdote.

The Big Picture

We are at a point in time when new work models have emerged and are promising sweeping changes, but government and society have not quite caught up. At the same time as the Gig Economy gets so much press and there is such concern about the employment status of Uber drivers, politicians and economists constantly bring up the issue of jobs in America. No one in power appears to be making the connection between the increase in alternative work arrangements and the decreased rate of traditional job growth. I find it fascinating that so few have tried to add alternative work arrangements into the overall "jobs" picture, but as of yet no one has.

Part of the problem, once again, is semantics. Just like people want to equate the sharing and Gig Economy, there is a similar problem with work in general, according to Eamonn Kelley, a managing director with Deloitte Consulting LLP and author of *Powerful Times*. He noted that Americans everywhere equate work and jobs, but work is so much more than a job, or more precisely a "regular full-time job."[7] SIC codes and other occupational classifications systems no longer describe the type of work that is done today. Work encompasses all sorts of pursuits, from part-time work to self-employment to gigs to volunteering.

Merriam-Webster defines *work* as "an activity in which one exerts strength or faculties to do or perform something."[8] In fact, in all 11 definitions cited, the word *employment* never appears. Work does not equal job.

What is unfortunate about this focus on jobs and not work is the attachment of social infrastructure to employment. What many people do not realize is that this association of benefits to employment is a fairly recent development. It dates back to what is often referred to as the Treaty of

Detroit, when in 1950, the United Auto Workers' Union agreed to a long-term contract in exchange for comprehensive benefits programs. The program was so successful, it became a model for other large corporation to use to structure their workforces. Since then, the extension of health and retirement benefits to employed workforces has become an expectation for many.

Employment also involves a host of regulations, from wage and hour laws to retirement and ERISA regulations to health and welfare regulations. Not surprisingly, given the governmental disinclination toward collaboration, the definition of an employee differs in these regulations, so some rules do not apply to all classes of workers. As the authors of *Lead the Work* so aptly point out:

> Interestingly, many of the problems addressed by existing labor laws may be less important in a free agent world. Certainly issues like unduly long working hours, unfair time-off policies, and arbitrary dismissal seem moot for free agents who make decisions about what work to do and when to work. Unsafe working conditions and discrimination are less likely to be problems when so much work is virtual and often done at the free agent's location of choice.[9]

In the long term, let us hope that the policy-makers catch up with the new ways of working. In the meantime, here is what we can expect at the macroeconomic level.

Independent Contractor Regulations

The spate of lawsuits involving Uber drivers has brought new attention to the somewhat arcane area of employment law that addresses the classification of independent contractors and employees. As discussed in Chapter 7, this area of the law is ambiguous, outdated, and in need of revision to reflect and enable a modern knowledge economy. Several ideas have been articulated as ways to rationalize the current structure.

The Hamilton Project of the Brookings Institution brings together economic and business thought leaders to research and advance proposals that would enhance the United States promise of opportunity and prosperity. In December 2015, it issued "A Proposal for Modernizing Labor Laws for Twenty-First Century Work: The 'Independent Worker,'" written by professors Seth Harris of Cornell and Alan Krueger of Princeton. The authors argue that the new digital talent platforms create an intermediary role that renders the worker participants in these platforms neither employees nor independent contractors. This is due in large part to the fact that the ongoing success of the intermediary is dependent on the worker. Unlike other definitions of employment, in which the worker's efforts are essential to the continuation of the company's business, in the digital platform world, the intermediary in addition to the company is reliant on these workers.[10]

The Independent Worker proposal attempts to neutralize the difference between employees and independent workers. The authors point to the distortions in the labor marketplace created by the uncertainty around the existing laws that have led to abuse of independent contractor status from some hiring companies in the interest of limiting employer obligations. Similarly, intermediaries, not wanting to appear as employers, have not extended certain features to their platform participants, features that would make the marketplace more efficient and provide true value to the independent workers.

The proposal calls for intermediaries to be able to provide pooled services for workers, so that they can offer access to benefits programs at group rates, making them more affordable to the independent workers. The payment technology embedded in these platforms would enable premium payments to be deducted from the gig fees due to the workers, thereby simplifying the process. Additionally, these technological capabilities would also enable these platforms to facilitate tax-withholding payments for the independent workers, which would significantly reduce the administrative burden on the workers and accelerate payments to the government. (Because, as I mentioned in Chapter 7, it's all about taxes, lawmakers should welcome this idea.) Other provisions would include the extension of civil rights protections to workers. Currently, independent contractors, freelancers, or independent workers of any kind would have no standing to bring a federal claim of discrimination, whether on gender, age, or disability. A final provision would extend collective bargaining rights to independent workers.

The authors argue that this proposal should be considered for legislation by Congress to change federal law. Because the existing law is so ineffective and applied across many different areas in different ways (e.g., the definition of an employee for OSHA purposes is different than for IRS purposes), an omnibus law enacted by Congress that uniformly addresses all of these issues would be the most efficient way to enact change

Although the paper had many advocates and critics when it was first released, no progress was made on legislation in 2016. However, it stands as a blueprint for future potential action.

Another interesting model is the Certified Self Employed Worker designation being advanced by MBO Partners. This construct is that in the absence of clear classification guidelines, a certification procedure could be put in place that establishes a worker as a self-employed independent contractor. In return for that designation, the worker would voluntarily waive the rights that typically accrue to employees. The procedure would be akin to a licensing process and the Small Business Administration would oversee it. Once certified, the designation would last for three years, at which time a renewal process could allow it to be extended. Again, no legislative progress has been made with this idea, but it is out there as another business model to be considered.

THE POLITICAL CRYSTAL BALL

Many predictions have been offered about how the Trump administration may act on the independent contractor issue. Secretary of Transportation Elaine Chao, a former Labor Undersecretary, is an advocate for rationalization of these regulations. She recently said, "Many of the government's workplace regulations were created during an era when workers spent the majority of their lives in one establishment or one profession. That's no longer the case today. So it is legitimate to ask if the regulatory solutions of the past—crafted by big government for big business—are appropriate for a peer-to-peer economy that is fluid, flexible and filled with workers who prefer independent arrangements."[11]

In a recent webinar, Jeff Wald, the cofounder of WorkMarket, a workforce automation software company, made his predictions about what the new Trump administration will mean for the On-Demand Economy.[12] He suggested that regulations, especially those resulting from the 2010 Obama task force meant to tackle independent contractor misclassification, would be discontinued or not enforced. Moreover, he thought the task force would be disbanded immediately, which would suggest there will be fewer compliance actions in the near term.

The nomination of Alexander Acosta, a former NLRB Board member and currently the dean of the law school at Florida International University as the Trump administration Secretary of Labor does not signal any clear policy direction. Acosta is viewed in the press as a lifelong Republican, competent manager, and career civil servant, so it can only be assumed that he will further the president's agenda to reduce the burden of regulation. Certainly the DOL has more than its share of regulations that could be culled.

Looking into his crystal ball for 2018, Wald thought there could be some movement in the chronic problem of worker classification. Trump likes to simplify complexity, and the rules governing independent contractor compliance are nothing if not complex.

The new administration will also have the opportunity to appoint a new commissioner for the National Labor Relations Board (NLRB). A recent NLRB decision adversely affected the staffing industry by increasing the risk of co-employment for companies using temporary staffing/gig workers. A new NLRB appointee could reverse that decision, which would be a boon for temporary and specialty staffing firms.

Finally, tax reform will likely take until 2018, because it is a complex problem. Again, in the interest of simplification, the new tax regulations could eliminate many of the business deduction provisions that have been a mainstay of the self-employed career consultants. That said, a lot will happen between now and then. Time to strap on for the ride.

The Social Safety Net

The biggest concern about the growth of the Gig Economy is the access to benefits typically afforded to employees. These include not just medical benefits and pensions, but also vacation pay, minimum wage, sick days, family leave, and insurance coverage for on-the-job injuries.

For those independent workers at the high end of the expertise pyramid, many of these issues are not a concern; the income earned by the successful independents enable them to create personal safety net structures. However, for those just starting out in the gig world as well as that minority cohort that are not working this way by choice, these issues are of deep concern and need to be addressed at a societal and policy level. Pundits in the field agree that many low-skilled workers may not be able to succeed in the new world of work. Already some new models are emerging that may be able to provide the needed support to any independent worker.

In November 2015, 38 prominent technology entrepreneurs, venture capitalists, academics, and policy-makers (including the founders of Care.com and Lyft, and the CEOs of Handy, Peers.org, and Instacart) released an open letter entitled "Common Ground for Independent Workers: Principles for Delivering a Stable and Flexible Safety Net for All Types of Work." They make the united argument that work has fundamentally changed, such that many alternative workers no longer have access to a social safety net, and it would benefit our country and our economy to develop a solution that provides stability and flexibility for workers.

They argue for a portable benefits vehicle that would be independent of an employer. To the extent that workers have several income sources, these portable benefits would be prorated by the fees earned at a given source. These benefits offerings should also be universal; in any role from free agent to long-term contractor to employee, one would have access to a common set of benefits.

This influential group did not offer specific suggestions; rather, they wanted to get the dialogue started: "With the same spirit of enterprise and mission, we invite policymakers and organizations to continue this conversation and contribute ideas."[13]

One of their members, however, has already moved forward on this idea. Care.com, a digital talent marketplace for caregivers and babysitters, has created an innovative "caregiver benefit" for its workers. Clients pay a small surcharge that finances a $500 cash benefit, "Care Benefit Bucks," which can be used by the worker for healthcare, transportation, or education.[14] Hopefully more companies will also follow suit.

And another member is involved with new legislation that is expected to be introduced in New York state in 2017. Handy, a digital platform for handymen and household workers, along with Tech NYC, a New York state trade association, is introducing a portable benefits bill Gig Economy workers.[15] The proposed voluntary program envisions a 2.5-percent fee payed by participating companies into a benefits fund. Workers could access the fund to purchase benefits, whether health insurance or pensions. The catch, according to some, is that the bill defines the workers as independent contractors, effectively cutting these gig workers off from employment benefits like overtime. The bill's proponents point to the need for incremental progress toward the goal of improving the social safety net.

PROFILE: SHIFTPIXY

Along with these efforts of entrepreneurs to change legislation, there are entrepreneurs who are just looking at the problems differently and in so doing providing a solution. Take the digital platform ShiftPixy as an example. ShiftPixy is a highly specialized platform that was introduced in a talent segment that most people would overlook: shift workers in the restaurant business. This low-paid, mostly minimum wage cohort that works for fast food chains, franchisors, and mom and pop operations is not one that attracts large-scale technology investment. That said, it is large and fragmented. According to ShiftPixy cofounder Steve Holmes, he and his partner saw the opportunity to create an app that could add efficiency to both sides of the marketplace; the app could schedule these workers, many of whom needed to pick up extra shifts to make ends meet, as well as meet the needs of many restaurant proprietors to maintain full staffing levels. More importantly, ShiftPixy employs the gig workers on behalf of its clients. By employing them, it enables them to accrue enough part-time hours from various clients to qualify for benefits typically only accorded to full-time employees. It is creating portable benefits for its employee pool. Not surprising to me, ShiftPixy is poised to go public later this year.

Another vulnerability for independent workers is the lack of on-the-job liability insurance. Independent contractors are not typically covered by workers' compensation insurance. There is one existing model, the Black Car Fund, that, as the Aspen Institute notes, could provide inspiration for new approaches. The Black Car Fund, founded in 1999, was originally designed for the limo drivers in New York City, most of whom were independent contractors without access to workers' compensation insurance. Now it includes more than 33,000 drivers including those that drive for Lyft and Uber. The Black Car fund charges a 2.5-percent surcharge on all rides provided by member entities, and the surcharge funds claims payments.[16]

Aside from this, though, there is still great uncertainty around independent contractors and insurance protections. (In fact, the ambiguity around independent contractor classifications looms large in the insurance industry.) In this case, there is a great example of innovation from a creative entrepreneur who knows that the problems in the insurance marketplace are not likely to be resolved soon. Chad Nitschke, CEO of Bunker Insurance, a digital platform for small business insurance for both contractors and clients, saw the problem with workers' compensation coverage, so developed a product to meet the need. Although not a pure workers' compensation policy, the product covers virtually the same types of workplace-related incidents that a traditional policy would cover. As of this writing, it is being piloted for two different talent platforms, one for construction workers and another for healthcare professionals—two groups that could be subject to potentially significant on-the-job-injuries. The product development process has been complicated, since individual states regulate insurance coverages. Nonetheless, they have secured an A-rated insurer, and the coverage is reasonably priced, as low $1/day. My guess is that when it is ready to launch nationwide, Bunker Insurance will have a ready market for its innovative product.[17]

The issue of paid time off is a bit more daunting. Although many have suggested it should be addressed at a policy level, it requires more individual attention. In fact, we all should remember that paid time off is not a statutory benefit; rather it is a voluntary benefit that many employers choose to offer. As such, independent workers can choose to budget for paid time off and even elect to create a separate funded account for it. Techniques abound at websites like Policygenius.com. In fact, there is now an app, Even, which helps users smooth their income streams.

Another safety net of sorts is the protection from deadbeat clients who do not pay their bills. The New York City Council passed a bill in November 2016, the Freelance Isn't Free Act, which supports freelancers who are stiffed by their clients, requiring penalties of up to $25,000 for chronic offenders. It is unclear if other jurisdictions will adopt similar legislation, but it does show major civic support for the independent workforce.

Finally, as noted earlier, the growth of this gig workforce is not just a U.S. phenomenon. As it grows globally, other countries are experiencing the challenges of major structural changes that come from a profound change in work patterns. Uber lost its first battle in Great Britain, when the courts declared in October 2016 that drivers could be considered employees and therefor eligible for holiday pay and pension benefits. In Singapore, a digital platform startup, MyWork, has devised a solution to the lack of a social safety net for gig workers by incorporating an optional charge to clients to cover the CPF, the Singaporean version of Social Security.[18] Hopefully, as many countries and companies worldwide devise solutions to some of the problems that have arisen, best practices can be shared.

Larger Policy Questions

There are many other ways that the increased growth in the Gig Economy will affect our economy and our culture. With people working fewer or greater hours in the Gig Economy, the unemployment calculation used by the government may be less accurate. Should gig workers be counted in the unemployment or employment side of the equation? Alternatively, is a whole new set of terminology required to describe the new world of work? The authors of The Solo City Report suggest, "We need new definitions that reflect the infinite variety of work arrangements that exist and the speed with which individuals move in and out of those arrangements. We need a new dynamic typology of work."[19]

Our understanding of the cyclical nature of employment around business cycles may also shift, as workers secure additional work through digital platforms during downtimes, a practice that did not exist 30 years ago. Valleys in these cycles may not be as deep, given the availability of project-based gigs. A recent Chicago Tribune article reported that one Uber driver said he would have had to go on food stamps, were it not for his Uber gigs. As economists grapple with what new terminology may be appropriate for the fundamental shifts in the economy, they may also need to search for a new normal in the data; historical comparisons may have less value as we go forward.

As more people become long-term gig workers with variable income, the housing market could be affected. Twenty years ago at M Squared, we often had to provide income verification for independent consultants seeking a mortgage. We explained that the income was based on projects and not an annual salary, so was not assured for future years. Interestingly, no regular job is assured for future years, either, but there is nonetheless an aura of permanence. Still today, many lenders are uncomfortable with what they see as an unstable income stream even from the most highly compensated independent workers. As such, financial institutions may be less likely to grant mortgages. Similarly, individuals who have satisfied a desire for flexibility may decide they do not want the fixed obligation of a mortgage payment, so preferences for home ownership could shift.

However, America is an entrepreneurial country. Chances are some creative entrepreneur will see this marketplace distortion and create a mortgage product for real property that doesn't require W2 income. The financial industry is replete with examples of innovative new products, but most have been done for the benefit of the issuers, the banks, and in-surance companies. What is needed is a product designed around the cus-tomer's needs. Perhaps it could even be structured to adjust, not at the behest of the institution based on the underlying reference rates, but on the request of the borrower based on his or her variable income stream. I, for one, am eager to see what develops.

Finally, with an optimistic perspective, certain experts have suggested that the growing Gig Economy could become a needed economic boost for the refugee community. As more and more people become displaced around the world, refugee camps are becoming a more permanent fixture. A critical need for the residents is to generate income. Performing project work that can be done remotely in the camp could provide such income. Samasource, a non-profit that brings technology skills to the poor to lift them out of poverty, is already trying to provide such job-brokering ser-vices. It could be that those efforts, coupled with a technology infrastruc-ture, from internet ready devices to virtual banking, could provide much needed assistance to this vulnerable population.

Chapter 10 Key Takeaways

- Technology, demographic trends, and workers' preferences for more flexibility are fueling the continued growth of the Gig Economy.

- Work is not synonymous with jobs. Work embraces many more types of productive pursuits.

- New models are being advanced to rationalize independent contractor compliance. The two key ideas are the Independent Worker Proposal and the Certified Self-Employed designa-tion. Either of these two models may be used to help simplify current labor market regulations.

- Portable benefits, which would be prorated by the amount earned from an income source, are being advanced by tech gurus and pundits alike as an important policy idea to ensure a social safety net for independent workers. Some progressive digital talent firms are beginning to implement such programs.

- The incoming Trump administration may fundamentally change some regulations that impede the Gig Economy related to independent contractor classification and others that enable it, such as the Affordable Care Act.

- Innovations to issues in the Gig Economy workplace may come from entrepreneurial companies impatient for the legal and regulatory issues to be resolved.

- Increased growth in the Gig Economy will have an impact on our society in other ways such as economic measurement.

11

The Future of the Gig Economy, Part 2: The Workplaces and the Workers

Futurestep, a talent division of Korn Ferry, one of the world's largest and most respected executive search firms, goes on record each year with its list of the top talent trends on the horizon. Its number-one trend for 2017 is "The Rise of the Gig Economy, or 'Me Inc'."[1] For some companies, the authors suggest, this will be a strategic shift, from "I need to hire someone" to "I need to get a project completed." Being named as the top trend heralds a new awareness of the gig world. More companies will be adopting this work mode, some with great difficulty, and more workers will be opting in to the independent lifestyle. A recent Upwork study, Freelancing in America, looked at the psychographic elements of the trend, citing the fact that 60 percent of independent workers said freelancing has become more respected as a career choice,[2] a perception that bodes well for continued growth. So what might that mean for both businesses and workers? Let's explore the implications in the near term, and then go out on a limb for some long-term thoughts.

"The future's so bright, I gotta wear shades."

—Timbuk3

The Business Issues

The recent Randstad study, Workplace 2025, defined independent professional workers as agile workers (why they had to invent yet another term, I do not know) and found the corporate marketplace deploying these resources more than one and a half times more frequently than they had just four years before. That is a growth rate of about 155 percent.[3]

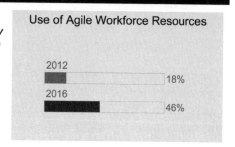

Agile Workforce Model*

Definition: The strategic ability to meet talent needs through real time use of contract, temporary, consulting, or freelance workers

Use of Agile Workforce Resources

2012   18%

2016   46%

*Source: Randstad, Workplace 2025

As the Gig Economy becomes even more prevalent in businesses of all sizes, the work environment itself will change. Contractors and freelancers will be working alongside regular employees on mission-critical projects. Long-term projects may well be done all or in part by non-employees who will not be there in the long term but are the best to get the job done now. Having the best workers to get the job done will become even more of an imperative, as the frictions associated with obtaining just the right expertise diminish in the evolving world of work. You need to have that right team, because if you don't, your competitor will. At the same time, you need to recognize that the motivations of that independent worker could be very different from the employee he/she is sitting beside.

New Worker Paradigm

Employees	Independents
Paid a salary	Paid for performance
Work in the office	Work anywhere
Use company equipment	BYOD*
Climb corp ladder	Be your own boss
Goal - Promotion	Goal - Expertise
Long-term view	No set horizon

*Bring Your Own Device

So to make this work effectively, companies will need to be prepared to onboard independent workers quickly and efficiently. This should include contractual obligations, fee payment processes, a technology orientation (to the extent the worker is participating in a custom technology environment of some sort), and some kind of overview of the company, department, and/or project.

All of these tasks can now be handled by a new segment of technology firms in the talent management space. For years, logistics companies have thrived by developing innovative products to manage a company's supply chain. Now the supply chain that needs to be managed is the talent supply chain. Talent management platforms, such as WorkMarket, provide an end-to-end solution for all aspects of the enterprise talent supply chain. They source independent workers, maintain the associated contracts, and automate the contract provisions to ensure that requirements like a nine-month end date, cannot be overlooked. These systems also handle independent contractor compliance, performing an assessment of the worker and the work before the fact.

Some, including Shortlist, offer "agile talent sourcing" on the platform. If a client needs to find a very specific expertise set, such as a copywriter who can translate Tagalog and has experience in beauty and cosmetics, Shortlist will partner with other platforms to identify the resource. As such, it will become the directory of directories for talent. This capability will be an internal one for their clients, thereby building the ability for these companies to quickly react to changes in the talent marketplace.

Similarly, the real innovation in the talent supply chain, though, has come with the advent of talent communities. These enable companies to maintain their own captive talent marketplace. When a company finds a good consultant, chances are they would be happy to engage him or her for another project. The talent community structure enables firms to maintain a database of the various independent workers who have been previously engaged company-wide. Performance ratings and details about the type of project worked, prior project manager, and other qualitative data are typically available. Digital talent platform Upwork also offers these communities and refers to it as a "Private Talent Cloud." These communities enable a more permanent connection with your preferred independent workers, workers who may be off to another client at any time.

The notion of a revolving door, in which key talent may walk out at any point in time, is one companies have wrestled with for years, but now it is becoming far more tangible. For many, especially those in the human resources (HR) field, this represents a very different approach to human capital. One of the most studied metrics in the HR world is turnover. Typically, a high rate of turnover is seen as a negative KPI, or key performance indicator. In the new workplace of gig workers and employees, turnover will become a very different metric. The KPI may be the return rate of your preferred consultants.

For in truth, people will come into an organization and develop an expertise. Many will remain, but others will become independent consultants offering their skills in the marketplace. In time, that same worker may return to your workplace as a free agent or an employee with even more sophisticated skills. This portfolio career path is not consistent with the old notions of turnover and it will be happening more and more frequently. In fact, certain technology companies are developing behavioral metrics to be able to identify when an employee is likely to leave the firm. The company uses this information to create an off-boarding process, that leaves the departing employee with a strong sense of connection to their former employer, a connection that could pay dividends in the future.

Companies need to take this a step further and recognize that part of the role of an employer is changing. Employers need to help train the next generation of independent workers, providing the management and leadership expertise that will enable them to create their own careers. Technology giant Cisco is already doing this by affording employees opportunities to work like a free agent on project teams composed of employees and contractors.[4]

Thirty-five years ago, Irish economist Charles Handy noted that the role of the corporation was one of being a career launcher. Raw talent comes in and the enterprise shapes it and develops it, to the point where she can go off on her own. In his book, *The Age of Unreason*, he likens the role to that of the British army: unskilled recruits come in, some remain, but most go off to other careers. Because there are only so many generals, everyone understands from the get-go that only the rare few will proceed up the ranks. Those who exit take with them some skills, a degree of polish, and a modicum of professional development that enables them to succeed in other organizations. His vision may be an even more accurate assessment of the role of the corporate world today than when he wrote that book more than 35 years ago. By training the next generation of independent workers, the enterprise sets itself up to become the beneficiary of their expanded expertise in the future.

However, developing a talent strategy to deploy alumni does have some complexity. There is the question of how a flexible career path will jive with retirement and benefits programs. For example, when Mary comes back as an employee after four years on her own, where she has developed a unique expertise that makes her hiring a coup, is she a *new* employee or not? Does her prior service count in terms of vesting schedules for stock options or eligibility periods for pension programs? Companies that want to thrive in the Gig Economy need to sort out these issues now in their talent acquisition strategies, before they become potential obstacles to the free flow of talent in the marketplace.

Because companies need a marketplace for talent to ensure they can procure the best resources. In that marketplace, they build their brand in hopes that the best resources will want to work for them. Given the war for talent right now, companies are very focused on this for their employees. They want to be the employer of choice. They want their employment brand to be the best it can be. But what about their consulting brand? Companies need to be thinking about not just being the employer of choice, but being the client of choice as well. The same talent management systems that enable greater efficiency for companies in managing all aspects of the workforce will make independent workers even more mobile. The best independent worker will be able to make his or her move to the company that is known to be the best place to work for consultants and contractors—that client of choice.

Becoming the client of choice will have certain non-negotiables. Regular and timely payment of fees will be critical. The Freelancer's Union recently had a series of bus and subway advertisements with the slogan "Your 90 day pay cycle doesn't match my 30 day rent cycle." Companies need to become more attuned to the fact that their payables are now going to individuals, and stretching those could have adverse consequences.

More senior consultants who can be considered legitimate independent contractors (potential legal changes notwithstanding) will appreciate being able to conduct business on a 1099 basis. Given the number of risk-averse companies that stopped engaging legitimate independent 1099 consultants, many of these individuals who had invested in creating a defensible 1099 structure were not able to use it. They either walked away from the business or agreed to do it on a W2 basis. These high-end consultants would welcome the chance to be paid in the way they designed their businesses to operate.

Access to opportunities to expand skills is also key to becoming a preferred client. Training programs are great opportunities to build connections with independent workers, because many free agents do not have access to such programs. Some firms use the Everwise talent platform, for example, to provide mentors at other companies for employees. Extending such a service to valued contractors would build tremendous goodwill.

Most importantly, perhaps, companies will have to develop a "plug and play" mindset that recognizes the different goals of the free agent workers. One trend that must be supported, for example, is the dual worker. In many disciplines, data scientists and cyber security specialists, for example, workers will want to combine employment—which could be full time—with outside projects. Most of the cybersecurity experts on the digital talent platform StealthHire are employed somewhere, but who take the cyber gigs on the side to make extra money because they are the only people are qualified to do the work. Interestingly, I was just interviewed by a freelance journalist who professed not to know about the Gig Economy, so I explained that he was part of it, because he had a contract to do an article on the gig world. He, too, was one of these dual career professionals: As well as being a freelance journalist, he is an employee partner in a PR agency in Atlanta. The gig article will broaden his knowledge of a key new subject that will help him add value to his firm. Hopefully he will also recognize that he is indeed a member of the Gig Economy.

However, it would not be fair to suggest that the world is moving relentlessly toward this plug-and-play future powered by the digital talent world. There could certainly be some bumps along the road. Already, several very well-financed platforms have closed their doors. In fact, 2016 was a record year for failures of digital platform companies. Some of the high-profile shuttered companies include Sidecar, a ride hailing service that was quickly eclipsed by Uber and Lyft; Shuddle, a ride service for busy parents who needed to transport children to playdates and sports; and Spoonrocket, a gourmet food delivery service. Just those three represented more than $70 million in funding.[5]

There are many reasons players in the platform economy could fail, including[6]:

- Interaction failure. If there are no cars when you want an Uber, you might not try again.

- Engagement issues. Participants take part a few times but do not remain as suppliers or customers. Three of the eight platforms I joined have sent me requests to come back to the platform and reengage.

- Match quality. If you cannot find the resource you are looking for, why would you go back? Certain platforms are adding concierge services to help clients find resources, a strategy that I imagine is to counter this issue.

- Negative network affair. Participants who exhibit bad behavior could ruin the experience for everyone. The story of the Uber driver who allegedly assaulted a passenger certainly had some adverse effects on patronage.

But long term, we must acknowledge that the entire world will be connected. Stephen De Witt, the CEO of WorkMarket, believes this will lead to a time when the algorithmic models will be able to deliver just the right talent automatically. The traditional intermediaries will be put out of business. To imagine the future, you need to think of the futures you know, so he frequently uses *Star Trek* as an analogy. "If Captain Kirk is in need of new expertise to make the next voyage," Stephen asked me, "do you think he is just going to list the job on LinkedIn?"[7]

That said, other pundits see the role of the intermediaries becoming even more central in organizations. The authors of *Lead the Work*, for example, see that the increased precision required to locate, onboard, and compensate mobile high-end talent will require very talented intermediaries. Because it is a staffing company, it is not surprising that the Randstad, in its Workforce 2025 report, also saw the increased primacy of the intermediary function in the workplace.

Clearly, companies are starting to organize for the new reality of a very eclectic workforce of free agents and employees. New job titles are springing up as a result. *Chief people officer* has already become a trendy term, but now there are also *freelance development officers* and *free agent wranglers*. (I love that last one.) One suggestion (of which I am not a fan) is "Workplace Engineering," to "reflect the new focus and a new mandate to create an optimally designed eco system of workers and workplaces to achieve the organization's mission."[8]

The Future for Workers

For those considering the independent life, the future seems bright. According to the MBO Partners 2016 State of Independence study, that includes about 29 million Americans over the age of 21. Adding in the nearly 40 million who are already in the independent workforce suggests a significant number of participants in the Gig Economy of the future.

My advice for individuals and how they should design a successful career in the evolving world of work takes a life style approach.

For those staring their career, education is key. It used to be learning engineering, marketing, or finance was a great way to launch a career. Now entrepreneurship is key. If you are to be the "CEO of Me," you need to know how to run your business. I apologize for my entrepreneur's bias, but this is true for all people, even those who are launching a career in medicine, geophysics, or academia. To earn extra money as you pursue your career education, given the increasing prevalence of digital talent platforms, you could become an occasional independent. In my informal surveys of Uber drivers, one lament came from a teacher who drove on the side. He had only ever been a W2 employee, so had no sense of what it meant to be an independent worker. He wished that Uber had given him a one-page document on "how to make the most money with Uber," so that he was more prepared to deduct his business expenses. No one should be in a position not to know how to navigate these career situations.

As an aside, I think our education system needs to catch up to this development. The Solo Project was an effort launched by the founders of *Inc.* magazine and *Fast Company* as well as the Knight Foundation to explore the solo worker movement and its attendant civic, societal, and policy implication. In their Solo City Report for 2016, they suggested that entrepreneurship education should start in fourth grade. If that isn't possible, basic entrepreneurship should be taught in high school as well as college to all students. A barebones curriculum would include some accounting and tax basics, branding, communications, and basic sales training. More aggressive programs could include organizational and/or psychometric content to facilitate emotional intelligence, hiring frameworks, and fundraising basics. The Kaufman Center for Entrepreneurial Leadership offers several programs, including a campus initiative aimed at bringing such a curriculum to community colleges. The programs are there; we just need to distribute them more widely.

If you don't have the opportunity to study entrepreneurship in school, you need to learn it on your own. As the 2016 Solo City Report said, we need to "teach students to *create* jobs, not find them,"[9] a skill that is based on entrepreneurial thinking. Again, the Kaufman Center is a great place to start. In collaboration with the Khan Academy, it launched an entrepreneurship series that is regularly reaching 6 million students and includes lessons from accomplished entrepreneurs including Richard Branson. There are scores of other places on the web to learn more about the subject, so go learn it.

PROFILE: BOONLE

One fledgling digital talent platform is trying to be an educational entrée for new creative talent. Boonle, headquartered in Rochester, New York, was conceived as a place for new freelancers to gain experience in the Gig Economy workplace. Founder Antonio Calabrese has established a pilot program with specific design programs at the Rochester Institute of Technology, in which students can use Boonle as a launch pad for their independent freelance business. It is tough for a rookie to get gigs in places such as Upwork or Fiverr, Calabrese explains.[10] Boonle will be a boon to these new creative free agents who need to build a portfolio. Clients can use the student work or participate in a "VIP" site, where only those members with several successful Boonle engagements can bid on projects. Although it does not yet have entrepreneurship or business management classes, he thought such content would be a great addition in the future.

Another finding of the Solo City Project was the identification of the personal characteristics that help make an individual successful in the new world of work. The Gig Economy, with its entrepreneurial elements, flexibility, pace, and uncertainty, is not for everyone. The most important element, according to the report, is grit, the ability to accept setbacks, learn from your mistakes, and demonstrate resilience. Other key elements include a tolerance for ambiguity, collaboration skills, problem-solving abilities in both standard and creative realms, and a willingness to seek out help. Understandably, being savvy with networks and adroit with personal branding are also key elements. The complete list appears here:

Characteristics of Successful Gig Workers

GRIT

TOLERANCE FOR
AMBIGUITY

CREATIVE
PROBLEM
SOLVING SKILLS

COLLABORATION
SKILLS

BUSINESS
FINANCE
LITERACY

NETWORK
UNDERSTANDING

RESOURCEFULNESS
AT GETTING HELP

SELF-AWARENESS

PERSONAL
BRANDING

ABILITY TO LEARN
CONTINUOUSLY

BUSINESS
DEVELOPMENT
SKILLS

DESIGN
AWARENESS

COMMUNICATION
SKILLS

Source: The Solo City 2016 Report

For those early in a career, who may be in a first or second job, recognize the opportunities for career development that typically come only from employment. These are "soft skill" areas, such as managing people. As more of the workforce becomes independent, management skills will become less prevalent. Most of the Baby Boomer generation have been well trained in big companies, many of which no longer exist. Similarly, that training is less available than it had been. So when you have the opportunity to participate in training programs, especially leadership, communication, and/or conflict resolution, take advantage of those opportunities. Similarly, being trained in any of those soft skill areas that are characteristics of successful gig workers, such as collaboration or design thinking, would be of value as well.

For those just starting or those advancing independent careers, personal brand management is key. In addition to the ideas in Chapter 4, another thought is to build your brand as part of your life design strategy. "Designing Your Life," a Stanford business school course which has now been repurposed as a book by professors and tech entrepreneurs Bill Burnett and Dave Evans, is a great way to think about your brand. Is the work you are configuring yourself to secure the work that will bring you satisfaction and happiness?

Experienced independents need to be attuned to the travails of your clients in this new world of work. Small companies may be struggling to keep pace, whereas large firms may have difficulty adjusting to the plug and play nature of their new workforce. You will become more connected to your clients if you facilitate their deeper dive into the independent workplace. Understand the role of the intermediaries who may be monitoring the preferred vendor lists or building the talent communities to know how to best maintain connections to your clients. If need be, guide your clients through the independent talent world to help them become more adept at deploying the free agent workforce. You can also be a guide for those individual clients who may want to join the ranks of the independent workforce, as, given the portfolio nature of careers, that could very well happen.

For the veteran independent workers, there is much to share. Some have suggested that experienced independents should develop a crowdsourced Yelp-type service for clients, providing the reviews that would lead to a "Client of Choice" designation (how it makes money is another question). If such an initiative does occur, participate. Your viewpoint as a successful player in the Gig Economy helps perfect the picture of what is happening in the marketplace.

Similarly, rookie independent workers could learn a great deal from veterans about client management, business development, difficult conversations when projects go awry, or a host of other topics specific to running an independent practice. M Squared provides some degree of training to rookie consultants in the way it manages its projects. Chris Neal, a principal with the firm, notes that because many Millennials move around a great bit in their career, they haven't had the opportunity to have a mentor.[11] The M Squared "Transformation Practice" uses very seasoned project leaders so that more junior independent consultants can learn how to approach projects and manage clients.

Other than that, the pickings appear to be slim. There are no mentor sites for independent consultants, although I have suggested to Everwise that they create one. LinkedIn has its independent consultant group, but I, for one, have not found the discussion terribly robust. In your own personal professional organizations and/or digital communities there may be venues for you to offer your counsel to the up-and-coming generation of independent workers. The data suggests there will be a great deal of them joining the ranks of the Gig Economy workforce. Be sure to teach them how they can thrive.

Chapter 11 Key Takeaways

- Companies need to recognize the different characteristics of the independent workers.

- Firms need to be ready for a portfolio employee, who may enter as an employee, depart, and return years later as a consultant.

- Custom talent communities designed to enable firms to easily re-deploy successful free agents will make firms more effective.

- Dual careers blending employment and gigs will become more prevalent.

- Key skills for individuals to thrive in the Gig Economy include grit, a tolerance for ambiguity, communication skills, problem-solving skills, and facility with business and finance.

- Individuals need to train themselves on entrepreneurship to thrive.

- Veteran independent workers should consider mentoring new independent workers as well as their clients in the tricks of the trade.

Selected Intermediaries and Digital Platform Companies

This listing is not intended to be a comprehensive listing of all companies, as I know there could be many that did not make this list either because they are self-funded, outside of the United States and not on the radar screen, or already out of business. That said, the bolded entries denote more traditional intermediaries. Italics indicate those who are out of business. The source of the data is Crunchbase.com (accessed January 4, 2017) and augmented by company websites.

Company	Founded	Funding	Size	Primary focus
99 Designs	2008	$45 mil; Accel Partners	Over $1 mil freelance designers	Web design, graphic design platform with contest model
Agent Anything	2010	Undisclosed	Montreal based	An errand platform for college students
Axiom	1999	$28 mil in 2013	1,500 Employees in 11 offices	Tech-enabled legal services
BellHops	2013	$13.5 mil in 2015; Canaan partners led	Operates in 53 cities/college towns	Moving services done by college students

Company	Founded	Funding	Size	Primary focus
BloggMutt	2011	Undisclosed	10,000 free-lance writers	Develop content for blog posts for companies and agencies
Boonle	2014	Undisclosed	Startup	Enables entry-level freelance creatives to get a start
Business Talent Group	**2007**	**$8 mil in 2016; Next Equity lead**	**5 cities in US; Inc. 500 twice**	**Independent consulting projects**
Caviar	2013	$15 mil in VC	Acquired by Square; valued at $90 mil	Delivery from high-end restaurants
Cerius Executives	**2007**	**Privately held**	**More than 6,000 senior consultants operating in 27 countries**	**Interim managers and senior consulting roles**
Cha Cha Cha	2006	$100 mil in VC	Operations are waning	Offers answers to any question from "guides"
Clever	2009	Self-funded	8,000 bloggers	Social media influencer database
ClickWorker	2005	$14.2 mil in 2015	700,000 freelancers in 136 countries	Handles standardized tasks, taking surveys, translation, and doing research
CoachUp	2011	$9.4 mil; backed by NBA Warrior Steph Curry	13,000 trainers and 100,000 athletes	Matches young athletes to independent coaches
Consultants.com		Backed by Global Ventures LLC	In beta mode	Platform for consultants to build digital brands
ConsultNet	1996	Independent	1,500 consultants and 300 clients	IT and engineering project services

Company	Founded	Funding	Size	Primary focus
CreativeCircle	2008	Acquired by OnAssignment in 2015		Advertising and creative talent platform
Curb	2007	$10.7 mil in 8/14	60 cities	An Uber for cab drivers
Dolly	2013	$9.7 mil in two rounds in 2015	5 cities	A move anything app with vetted "helpers"
DoorDash	2013	$186.7 mil; Sequoia Capital lead	250 cities	Food deliveries from restaurants
Eden McCallum	**2000**	**Independent**	**1,500 projects, 500 consultants**	**Independent consulting firm with a network of consultants**
Everwise	2012	$26.3 mil; Sequoia Capital lead	250 enterprise clients	Talent development platform connects young talent with mentors
Experfy	2014	$1.5 mil	Largest data scientist training platform	Talent and training platform for data scientists
Expert 360 (Aus)	2012	$5.1 mil, Frontier Ventures lead	10,000 vetted freelancers, 87 countries	Consultants for projects
Fiverr	2010	$30 mil in 2014	Claims more than 300,000 gigs completed since 2010	Graphic design, websites, translation
Freelance (Aus)	2009	Public in AUS; market cap $455mil	22 mil registered users, 10 mil jobs posted	Platform for website development, graphic design, digital marketing mobile apps
Gengo	2008	$24.2mil from 24 investors	10,000 registered translators	Crowd-based translation services

Company	Founded	Funding	Size	Primary focus
Gerson Lehrman Group	1998	Unknown	500K thought leaders, 1,400 clients, 22 global offices	Consulting professionals for short-term projects
Gig Salad	2007	1 mil gig walkers	90,000 bands	Marketplace for entertainment for parties/events
Gigwalk	2010	$17.8 mil		Workplace management platform to manage gig and regular workers
Grub Hub	2004	NYSE, market cap $3.1 bill 1/3/2017	174K orders daily	Food delivery from restaurants
Guru	1998	$16 mil; acquired by Emoonlighter	1.5 mil members, 1 mil jobs completed	Freelance marketplace, Web design, IT, and administrative gigs
Handy	2012	$60.7 mil in five rounds	1 million bookings in 2015	Household help (plumbers, handymen, cleaners)
HourlyNerd	2013	$22 mil in 2016	10,000 consultants	Consulting platform for MBAs; 14.5% commission
Instacart	2012	$274 mil in five rounds	7K shoppers	Delivers groceries
Lyft	2012	$1 bil in VC	65 U.S. cities	Ride hailing
M Squared	**1988**	**Sold to Solomon Edwards in 2013**	**California-based**	**Consultants for projects as well as solutions consulting**
McKinley Marketing	**1995**	**Independent**	**Washington, DC–based**	**Consultants and contractors for marketing projects**

Company	Founded	Funding	Size	Primary focus
Mech Turk	2006	Owned by Amazon	Product in beta	Does "human intelligence tasks" that can't be done by computers (e.g., selecting pictures)
Medicast	2013	1.9 mil	FLA and SoCal	House call platform for docs
Munchery	2011	$120.4 mil in five rounds; Menlo Ventures and Sherpa	300 customers/wk. growing 20%/month	Delivers chef-crafted meals
Postmates	2011	$278.1 mil	20K active postmates; 40 major U.S. markets	Local on-demand food delivery; partners with restaurant chains
RedBeacon	2008	$7.4 mil	Purchased by Home Depot in 2012	Platform for household help, errands, and services
Samasource	2008	1.5 mil	Non-profit to help workers in developing world	Trains workers in basic skills and then platform offers gig work
Shift Pixy	2015	Currently considering an IPO	Operations largely in SoCal	Employment platform for restaurant workers
Shortlist	2014	$1 mil	Recently completed beta	Talent management marketplace
Shuddle	**2014**	**$12.2 mil**	**Closed after failing to get more funding**	**Ride service for parents needing to transport kids**
Shypp	2013	$62.1 mil	Valued at $240 mil by VentureBeat	Shipping platform, both commercial and residential
Skillshare	2010	22.75 mil	2 mil students $5 mil paid to teachers	Learning community for students; talent platform for teachers

Company	Founded	Funding	Size	Primary focus
Spare Hire	2013	1.75 mil	100K roles matched	Consulting platform focused on financially oriented roles
Spoonrocket	**2013**	**$13.5 mil**	**Closed in July 2016**	**High-quality meal delivery**
Sprig	2013	$56.7 mil	No indication	Delivery of healthy meals
Stealth Worker	2015	$120K; Y Combinator backed	Still in beta	Platform for data security experts
Taskrabbit	2008	$37.7 mil	Unclear; growth has stalled according to Bloomberg	App for everyday chores
Thumbtack	2009	$273 mil	$1 bil in gigs in 2015	Platform for household chores, painting plumbing, handymen
TopCoder	2001	$11.3 mil	Acquired by Appirio	IT development platform using crowdsourced resources
TopTal	2010	Undisclosed; 1 round 7 investors	No indication	Hire top 3% of Web experts, designers, and financial freelancers
Tripda	**2014**	**$17.2 mil**	**Shut down in 2016**	**Long-distance ride sharing**
Uber	2009	$8.7 bil	Est. $60+ bil market cap	Ride sharing
UpCounsel	2012	$14 mil	Touts itself as the largest legal platform	Platform to connect with in-house counsel
Upwork/ ework	2005	$74 mil	Touts itself as largest freelance marketplace	IT, Web development, junior marketing

Company	Founded	Funding	Size	Primary focus
Wonolo	2014	$7.9 mil	25,000 screened workers	On-demand staffing for day laborers
WorkMarket	2010	$41 mil	Touts itself as #1 talent management marketplace	Talent marketplace for managing contractors and freelancers
Zaarly	2011	$15.1 mil	In three major cities	Mobile app for handyman, house cleaning, lawn & garden
Zintro.com	2010	Undisclosed	220,000 specialized experts	Global platform for consulting gigs from projects to conversations

My Digital Platform Experience

My Platform Experience

	Breadth of Info	Vetting	Company Info	Gig Info	Activities	Gigs for Me
Consultants.com	○	○	○	○	✓	○
ExecRank	★	★	✓	★	★	✓
Gerson Lehrman	★	★	○	○	○	○
Hourly Nerd	✓	○	✓	✓	✓	✓
LinkedIn Pro	○	○	○	✓	○	✓
PWC	★	★	★	○	○	○
Quantifye	✓	✓	✓	○	○	○
Spare Hire	✓	✓	★	★	○	○

Legend

★ Always

✓ Sometimes

○ Seldom/not at all

Explanation

Here is my rating of the platforms I joined. Some only used a LinkedIn profile, while others requested more info. A few had further vetting processes. Company updates were sent by some. Additional ways to become engaged were actively promoted by one of the platforms. Available gig opportunities was a regular feature of some, although few gigs were appropriate for my skill set...at least so far.

Notes

Chapter 1

1. Dictionary.com, *www.dictionary.com/browse/gig?s=t.*

2. Steven Gill, "Good Riddance Gig Economy: Uber Ayn Rand and the Awesome Collapse of Silicon Valley's Dream of Destroying Your Job," *Salon,* March 27, 2016.

3. "The Global Economy Is Failing 35% of the World's Talent," *Exchange Magazine,* June 29, 2016.

4. MBO Partners, "State of Independence in America 2015," p. 14, *www.mbopartners.com/state-of-independence/ mbo-partners-state-of-independence-in-america-2015.*

5. Devin Coldewey, "Elizabeth Warren Takes on the So Called Gig Economy in a Speech," *Tech Crunch,* May 20, 2016.

6. Arun Sundarajan, *The Sharing Economy: The End of Employment and the Rise of Crowd Based Capitalism* (Cambridge, Mass.: The MIT Press, 2016), location 371 of 5185.

7. "Measuring the Gig Economy—Inside the New Paradigm of Contingent Work," Staffing Industry Analysts, Crain Communications, 2016.

8. Dianna Farrell and Fiona Greig, "Paychecks, Paydays and the Online Economy—Big Data on Income Volatility," JP Morgan Chase Institute, February 2016, *www.jpmorganchase.com/corporate/institute/document/jpmc-institute-volatility-2-report.pdf.*

9. Josh Zumbrun, "Most Americans Don't Know About Ride Sharing and the Gig Economy," *Wall Street Journal,* May 19, 2016.

10. "Measuring the Gig Economy," Staffing Industry Analysts, p. 2.

11. MBO Partners State of Independence in America 2015, p. 2.

Chapter 2

1. MBO Partners, "State of Independence in America Report 2016," p. 8, *www.mbopartners.com/blog/inside-the-2016-state-of-independence-in-america-from-mbo-partners.*

2. Sandararajan, *The Sharing Economy,* location 422 of 5185.

3. James Mayika, Susan Lund, Jaques Bughin, Kelsey Robinson, Jan Mischke, and Deepa Mahajan, "Independent Work— Choice, Necessity and the Gig Economy," McKinsey Global Institute, October 2016, p. 72.

4. Mayika, Lund, Bughin, Robinson, Mischke, and Mahajan, "Independent Work," p. 30.

5. Adam C. Uzialko, "The Gig Economy's Growing Influence on the American Workforce," *Business News Daily,* July 1, 2016.

6. Staffing Industry Analysts, "Measuring the Gig Economy," p. 4.

7. Chris Neal, interview with the author.

8. The Future of Work podcast, "Why the Gig Economy is the Future of Work," Episode 61, November 29, 2015.

9. "Digital Matching Firms: A New Definition in the 'Sharing Economy' Space," Office of the Chief Economist, Department of Commerce, June 3, 2016.

10. Mayika, Lund, Bughin, Robinson, Mischke, and Mahajan, "Independent Work," p. 37.

11. "Gig Economy Index," a PYMNTS.com Hyperwallet Collaboration, October 2016, p. 4.

12. Silke Trost, "Age Matters—Myths and Truths About AME Generational Lifestyles," Nielsen Global Report, September 15, 2014, *www.nielsen.com/pk/en/insights/news/2015/age-matters-myths-and-truths-about-ame-generational-lifestyles.html.*

13. MBO Partners, "State of Independence in America 2016," p. 3.

14. John Boudreau, Ravin Jesuthasan, and David Creelman, *Lead the Work: Navigating a World Beyond Employment* (Hoboken, N.J.: Jossey-Bass, 2016), location 1801.

15. MBO Partners, "State of Independence Study 2015," p. 6.

16. MBO Partners, "State of Independence in America Report."

17. Millennials in the Work Force, Intuit website, *payments.intuit.com/millennials-job-market/.*

18. MBO Partners, "State of Independence in America 2016," p. 8.

19. MBO Partners, "State of Independence in America 2015."

20. Ibid., p. 7.

21. Ibid., p. 8.

22. Ibid.

Chapter 3

1. Future of Work podcast, "Why the Future of Work Is all About People," Episode 93, July 11, 2016.

2. Boudreau, Jesuthasan, and Creelman, *Leading the Work*, location 2664.

3. "Small Agency Series: Hub Strategy and Communications," *The San Francisco Egotist,* October 5, 2016.

4. Email to the author from Mike Cappelluti, November 10, 2016.

5. A Connect website, *www.a-connect.com.*

6. Business Talent Group blog, *https://businesstalentgroup.com/blog.*

7. Susan Adams, "Little Passports Founders Desperately Wanted VC Cash. Luckily They Got Zero," *Forbes,* November 2, 2016.

8. "CFOs Turn to Consultants as Challenges Mount," *Wall Street Journal,* July 25, 2016.

9. John Dame, "How the Gig Economy Can Fit Your Business," *Central Pennsylvania Business Journal,* September 30, 2016.

10. Email to the author from Marc McConnaughey, October 12, 2016.

Chapter 4

1. Marion McGovern and Dennis Russell. *A New Brand of Expertise: How Independent Consultants, Free Agents and Interim Managers Are Transforming the World of Work.* (Woburn, Mass.: Butterworth Heinemann, 2001), Chapter 5.

2. "From Zero to Seventy (Billion)," *The Economist,* September 3, 2016, p. 19.

3. Presented in a speech to The Alliance of CEOs, attended by the author, November 11, 2016.

4. Jeremy Goldman and Ali B. Zagat, *Getting to Like: How to Boost Your Personal and Professional Brand to Expand Your Opportunities, Grow Your Business and Achieve Financial Success* (Wayne, N.J.: Career Press, 2016), location 384 of 3738.

5. "Fifty-Eight Percent of Employers Have Caught a Lie on a Resume, According to a New CareerBuilder Survey," Careerbuilder.com website, *www.careerbuilder.com/share/aboutus/pressreleasesdetail.aspx?sd=8%2F7%2F2014&id=pr837&ed=12%2F31%2F2014.*

6. Ibid.

7. Catherine Fisher, interview with the author.

8. Growing Social Media website, *http://growingsocialmedia .com/fastest-growing-social-media-networks.*

9. "Solo City 2016 Report," The Knight Foundation and The Solo Project, 2016, p. 44.

Chapter 5

1. Dennis Russell, *Interim Management* (Oxford, England: Butterworth Heineman, 1998), p. 55.

2. McGovern and Russel, *A New Brand of Expertise*, p. 106.

Chapter 6

1. "Interim Executive Confidential—The Interim Executive," Cerius Executives website, October 5, 2016, *https://ceriusexecutives.com/ interim-executive-confidential-independent-executive-4/.*

2. Diana Farell and Fiona Greig, "Paychecks, Paydays and the Online Economy—Big Data on Income Volatility," JP Morgan Chase Institute, p. 21.

3. David Evans and Richard Schmalensee, "The Business That Platforms Are Actually Disrupting," *Harvard Business Review*, September 21, 2016.

Chapter 7

1. IRS website, *www.irs.gov/pub/irs-utl/x-26-07.pdf.*

2. Heather Sommerville, "Uber Has Lost Again in the Fight Over How to Classify its Drivers," Reuters, September 10, 2015.

3. Mike Isaac, "Ruling Tips Uber Drivers Away From Class Action Suits," *New York Times*, September 7, 2016.

4. Stephen Gandal, "Ubernomics: Here's How Much It Would Cost for Uber to Pay its Drivers as Employees," *Fortune*, September 17, 2015.

5. "Vendor Management System," Wikipedia website, *https://en.wikipedia.org/wiki/Vendor_management_system*.

6. Francine McKenna, "PWC's California Overtime Case Settles, but the Big Four Business Model Will Change Anyway," *Bullmarket, https://medium.com/bull-market/pwc-s-california-overtime-case-settles-but-the-big-four-business-model-will-change-anyway-8598ce74c1da#.id9xohnif.*

Chapter 8

1. Email to the author, November 1, 2016.

2. Solo City 2016 Report, p. 14.

3. Sally Augustin, "Rules for Designing an Engaging Workplace," *Harvard Business Review*, October 2014.

Chapter 9

1. Freelancer's Union website, *www.freelancersunion.org/about/*.

2. Lucy Lupion and Jill Rosenberg, "Statutory Protections for Freelance Workers: New York City Paving the Way for a New Category of Worker?" JD Supra Business Advisor, November 3, 2016, *www.jdsupra.com/legalnews/statutory-protections-for-freelance-40459/*.

3. Ubiquity website, *www.myubiquity.com/educate/*.

4. The Hivery website, *www.thehivery.com/events/*.

5. "Top 100 Freelance Blogs," Upwork website, *www.upwork.com/blog/2009/04/top-100-freelance-blogs/*.

Chapter 10

1. Mayika, Lund, Bughin, Robinson, Mischke, and Mahajan, "Independent Work," p. 67.

2. MBO Partners State of Independence Study, 2016, p. 2.

3. "Randstad US Study Projects Massive Shift to Agile Employment and Staffing Model in the Next Decade," PR Newswire, *www.prnewswire.com/news-releases/randstad-us-study-projects-massive-shift-to-agile-employment-and-staffing-model-in-the-next-decade-300376669.html*.

4. Mayika, Lund, Bughin, Robinson, Mischke, and Mahajan, "Independent Work," p. 4.

5. This is a number that has been reported in multiple sources, among them Pew Research, AARP, and *The Washington Post*. Wayne Cascio also quoted it in his interview with the author.

6. Lael Brainard, "Evolution of Work," A Convening Co-sponsored by the Board of Governors of the Federal Reserve System, the Federal Reserve Bank of New York, and the Freelancer's Union, New York, NY, November 17, 2016.

7. Eamonn Kelley, interview with the author.

8. "Work." *Merriam-Webster*.

9. Boudreau, Jesuthasan, and Creelman, *Lead the Work*, location 5100.

10. Seth D. Harris and Alan B. Krueger, "A Proposal for Modernizing Labor Laws for Twenty-First Century Work: The 'Independent Worker'," The Hamilton Project, Brooking Institute, December 2015, p. 10.

11. Richard Menghello, "Sharing Economy Companies All Smiles After Trump's Transpo Pick," JD Supra Business Advisor, December 1, 2016.

12. Webinar hosted by WorkMarket, November 29, 2016, 2 p.m. EST.

13. "Common Ground for Independent Workers," Medium.com, November 9, 215, *https://medium.com/the-wtf-economy/common-ground-for-independent-workers-83f3fbcf548f#.rjitwyqmd.*

14. Abigail Carlton, Rachel Kornberg, Daniel Pike, and Willa Seldon, "The Freedom Insecurity and Future of Independent Work," *Stanford Social Innovation Review*, December 21, 2016.

15. Cole Stangler, "Uber, but for Benefits: NY Tech Companies Propose a Gig Economy Solution," *The Village Voice*, January 3, 2017.

16. Daniel Rolf, Shelby Clark, and Corrie Watterson Bryant, "Portable Benefits in the 21st Century," The Aspen Institute, 2016, p. 10.

17. Chad Nitschke, interview with the author.

18. Yasmine Yahya, "Managing the Gig Economy," *The Straits Times*, December 26, 2016, *www.straitstimes.com/business/economy/managing-the-gig-economy-economicaffairs.*

19. Solo City 2016 Report, p. 5.

Chapter 11

1. "Korn Ferry Futurestep Makes 2017 Talent Trend Predictions," Korn Ferry website, December 2016, *www.futurestep.com/news/korn-ferry-futurestep-makes-2017-talent-trend-predictions/.*

2. "New Study Finds Freelance Economy Grew to 55 Million Americans This Year, 35% of Total U.S. Workforce," Upwork press release, *www.upwork.com/press/2016/10/06/freelancing-in-america-2016/.*

3. Randstad, "Workplace 2025."

4. Future of Work podcast, "Why the Future of Work Is All About People," Episode 93, July 11, 2016.

5. Dara Kerr, "RIP to the On-Demand Companies That Fizzled in 2016," December 18, 2016, *www.cnet.com/news/rip-on-demand-companies-that-fizzled-shutdown-died-in-2016/.*

6. Marshall Van Alstyne, Geoffrey G. Parker, and Paul Choudary, "Pipelines, Platforms and the New Rules of Strategy," *Harvard Business Review*, April 2016.

7. Stephen De Witt, interview with the author.

8. Boudreau, Jesuthasan, and Creelman, *Lead the Work*, location 3195.

9. Solo City 2016 Report, *www.thesoloproject.com/the-quarterly/#new-page-1*, p. 33.

10. Antonio Calabrese, interview with the author.

11. Chris Neal, interview with the author.

Bibliography

Books

Boudreau, John, Ravin Jesuthasan, and David Creelman. *Lead the Work: Navigating a World Beyond Employment* (Hoboken, N.J.: Jossey-Bass, 2015). Kindle edition.

Evans, David S., and Richard Schmalensee. *The Matchmakers: The New Economics of Mulitsided Platforms* (Cambridge, Mass.: Harvard Business Review Press, 2016). Kindle edition.

Goldman, Jeremy, and Ali B. Zagat, *Getting to Like: How to Boost Your Personal and Professional Brand to Expand Your Opportunities, Grow Your Business and Achieve Financial Success* (Wayne, N.J.: Career Press, 2016). Kindle edition.

Handy, Charles. *The Second Curve: Thoughts on Reinventing Society* (London: Penguin Random House, 2015). Audible edition.

Horowitz, Sara, and Toni Sciarra Poynter. *The Freelancer's Bible* (New York: Workman Publishing, 2012). Kindle edition.

Kossek, Eileen Ernst, and Brenda A. Lautsch. *The CEO of Me* (New York: Pearson Education Limited, 2007). Kindle edition.

McGovern, Marion, and Dennis Russell. *A New Brand of Expertise: How Independent Consultants, Free Agents and Interim Managers Are Transforming the World of Work* (Woburn, Mass.: Butterworth Heinemann, 2001).

Sundarajan, Arun. *The Sharing Economy: The End of Employment and the Rise of Crowd Based Capitalism* (Cambridge, Mass.: The MIT Press, 2016). Kindle edition.

Articles

Adams, Susan. "Little Passports Founders Desperately Wanted VC Cash. Luckily They Got Zero." *Forbes,* November 2, 2016.

Augustin, Sally. "Rules for Designing an Engaging WorkPlace." *Harvard Business Review,* October 2014.

Brainard, Lael. "Evolution of Work," A Convening Co-Sponsored by the Board of Governors of the Federal Reserve System, the Federal Reserve Bank of New York, and the Freelancer's Union, New York. New York. November 17, 2016.

Carlton Abigail, Rachel Kornberg, Daniel Pike, and Willa Seldon. "The Freedom Insecurity and Future of Independent Work." *Stanford Social Innovation Review,* December 21, 2016.

"CFOs Turn to Consultants as Challenges Mount." *Wall Street Journal.* July 25, 2016.

Coldewey, Devin. "Elizabeth Warren Takes on the So Called Gig Economy in a Speech." Tech Crunch, May 20, 2016, *http://techrunch.com/2016/05/20/ Elizabeth-warren0takes-on-the-so-called-gig-economy-in-speech.*

Dame, John. "How the Gig Economy Can Fit Your Business. *Central Pennsylvania Business Journal,* September 30, 2016.

Evans, David, and Richard Schmalensee. "The Business That Platforms Are Actually Disrupting." *Harvard Business Review,* September 21, 2016.

Gandal, Stephen. "Ubernomics: Here's How Much it Would Cost for Uber to Pay its Drivers as Employees." *Fortune,* September 17, 2015.

Gill, Steven. "Good Riddance Gig Economy: Uber Ayn Rand and the Awesome Collapse of Silicon Valley's Dream of Destroying Your Job." *Salon,* March 27, 2016.

"The Global Economy Is Failing 35% of the World's Talent." *Exchange Magazine,* June 29, 2016.

Isaac, Mike. "Ruling Tips Uber Drivers Away From Class Action Suits." *New York Times,* September 7, 2016.

Kerr, Dara. "RIP to the On-Demand Companies That Fizzled in 2016." December 18, 2016. *www.cnet.com/news/ rip-on-demand-companies-that-fizzled-shutdown-died-in-2016/.*

Lupion, Lucy, and Jill Rosenberg. "Statutory Protections for Freelance Workers: New York City Paving the Way for a New Category of Worker?" JD Supra Business Advisor. *www.jdsupra.com/legalnews/ statutory-protections-for=freelnce-40459.*

McKenna, Francine. "PWC's California Overtime Case Settles, but the Big Four Business Model Will Change Anyway." *Bullmarket. https:// medium.com/bull-market/pwc-s-california-overtime-case-settles- but-the-big-four-business-model-will-change-anyway-8598ce74c1da#. id9xohnif.*

Menghello, Richard. "Sharing Economy Companies All Smiles After Trump's Transpo Pick." JD Supra Business Advisor, December 1, 2016.

Nolan, Hamilton. "The Gig Economy Is Growing and it's Terrifying." *Gawker,* March 31, 2016.

"PWC Launches an Online Marketplace to Tap the Gig Economy." *Financial Times,* March 6, 2016.

"Randstad US Study Projects Massive Shift to Agile Employment and Staffing Model in the Next Decade." PR Newswire. *www. prnewswire.com/news-releases/randstad-us-study-projects- massive-shift-to-agile-employment-and-staffing-model-in-the-next- decade-300376669.html.*

Rolf, Daniel, Shelby Clark, and Corrie Watterson Bryant. "Portable Benefits in the 21st Century." The Aspen Institute, 2016.

"Small Agency Series: Hub Strategy and Communications." *The San Francisco Egotist,* October 5, 2016.

Smith, Rebecca. "Most Benefits of the Gig Economy Are Completely Imaginary." *Quartz,* March 4, 2016.

Sommerville, Heather. "Uber Has Lost Again in the Fight Over How to Classify Its Drivers." Reuters, September 10, 2015.

Stabgker, Cole. "Uber, but for Benefits—NY Tech Companies Propose a Gig Economy Solution." *The Village Voice,* January 3, 2017.

Trost, Silke. "Age Matters: Myths and Truths About AME Generational Lifestyles." *Nielsen Global Report,* September 15, 2014. *www.nielsen.com/pk/en/insights/news/2015/age-matters-myths-and-truths-about-ame-generational-lifestyles.html.*

Uzialko, Adam C. "The Gig Economy's Growing Influence on the American Workforce." *Business News Daily,* July 1, 2016.

Van Alstyne, Marshall W., Geoffrey G. Parker, and Paul Choudary. "Pipelines, Platforms and the New Rules of Strategy." *Harvard Business Review,* April 2016.

Williams, David. "Skilled Professionals Will Dominate the Gig Economy, Report Says." *Small Business Trends,* March 17, 2016.

Yahya, Yasmine. "Managing the Gig Economy." *The Straits Times,* December 26, 2016. *www.straitstimes.com/business/economy/managing-the-gig-economy-economicaffairs.*

"From Zero to Seventy (Billion)." *The Economist,* September 3, 2016.

Zumbrun, Josh. "Most Americans Don't Know About Ride Sharing and the Gig Economy." *Wall Street Journal,* May 19, 2016.

———. "The Entire Online Gig Economy Might Be Mostly Uber." *Wall Street Journal,* March 28, 2016.

Reports

"Digital Matching Firms: A New Definition in the 'Sharing Economy' Space." Office of the Chief Economist, U.S. Department of Commerce, June 3, 2016.

Farrell, Dianna, and Fiona Greig. "Paychecks, Paydays and the Online Economy—Big Data on Income Volatility." JP Morgan Chase Institute, February 2016. *www.jpmorganchase.com/corporate/institute/document/jpmc-institute-volatility-2-report.pdf.*

"Gig Economy Index," a PYMNTS.com Hyperwallet Collaboration, October 2016. *www.hyperwallet.com/news-announcements/hyperwallet-gig-economy-index-unveils-worker-habits-preferences-future-goals/.*

Harris, Seth D., and Alan B. Krueger. "A Proposal for Modernizing Labor Laws for Twenty-First Century Work: The 'Independent Worker.'" The Hamilton Project, Brooking Institute, December 2015.

Mayika, James, Susan Lund, Jaques Bughin, Kelsey Robinson, Jan Mischke, and Deepa Mahajan. "Independent Work—Choice, Necessity and the Gig Economy." McKinsey Global Institute, October 2016.

"MBO Partners State of Independence in America 2015." *www.mbopartners.com/state-of-independence/ mbo-partners-state-of-independence-in-america-2015.*

MBO Partners. "6th Annual State of Independence Study." 2016, *www.mbopartners.com/state-of-independence/ mbo-partners-state-of-independence-in-america-2016.*

"Millennials in the Workforce." Intuit, *https://payments.intuit.com/ millennials-job-market/.*

Rolf, Daniel, Shelby Clark, and Corrie Watterson Bryan. "Portable Benefits in the 21st Century." The Aspen Institute. 2016.

"Solo City Report." The Knight Foundation and the Solo Project, 2016. *www.thesoloproject.com/the-report/.*

Staffing Industry Analysts. "Measuring the Gig Economy: Inside the New Paradigm of Contingent Work." Staffing Industry Analysts, Crain Communications, 2016.

Online Sources

A Connect, *www.a-connect.com.*

Business Talent Group blog. *https://businesstalentgroup.com/blog/.*

Careerbuilder.com. *www.careerbuilder.com/share/aboutus/ pressreleasesdetail.aspx?sd=8%2F7%2F2014&id=pr837&ed=12%2F31 %2F2014.*

Cerius Executives. *https://ceriusexecutives.com/ interim-executive-confidential-independent-executive-4/.*

Dictionary.com. *www.dictionary.com/browse/gig?s=t.*

Freelancer's Union. *www.freelancersunion.org/about/.*

The Future of Work Podcast. "Why the Future of Work Is All About People." Episode 93, July 11, 2016.

The Future of Work Podcast. "Why the Gig Economy Is the Future of Work." Episode 61, November 29, 2015.

IRS.gov. *www.irs.gov/pub/irs-utl/x-26-07.pdf.*

Korn Ferry website. *www.futurestep.com/news/ korn-ferry-futurestep-makes-2017-talent-trend-predictions/.*

MBO Partners blog. *www.mbopartners.com/resources/article/ paperwork-process-politics-government-contracting.*

Medium.com. *https://medium.com/the-wtf-economy/common-ground-for-independent-workers-83f3fbcf548f#.rjitwyqmd.*

Ubiquity. *www.myubiquity.com/educate/.*

Upwork. *www.upwork.com/blog/2009/04/top-100-freelance-blogs/.*

WorkMarket webinar. November 29, 2016, 2 p.m. EST.

Index

About the Author

Marion McGovern was one of the early entrepreneurs in the Gig Economy before that term was even coined. In 1988, she founded M Squared Consulting Inc. and grew it to a national enterprise, with offices in San Francisco, Los Angeles, and San Diego. M Squared Consulting Inc. was a niche-consulting firm that used its network of independent consultants to meet the needs of its clients, and was one of the first firms in the country to serve the virtual management marketplace. In 1995, she founded an affiliated company, Collabrus, to manage the employment compliance issues surrounding independent consultants, the very issue that has dogged the on-demand economy giant Uber.

In 1999, she sold M Squared to a public South African human capital company, the Kelly Group. In 2005, Marion hired a new CEO and became chairman. Four years later, the CEO left and the Kelly Group asked her to step back in as CEO on an interim basis. After a year in the role, righting the ship in the recession, Marion retired again. She remained a director through 2013, when the Kelly Group sold M Squared to a U.S. staffing firm, Solomon Edwards.

Marion has been a regular speaker and contributor on the subject of the workplace trends surrounding independent expertise. She was hailed as an innovator in Tom Peter's book, *Liberation Management.* She been featured in leading publications like *Fast Company, Fortune,* and *Forbes.* Marion was a regular speaker on the topic of workplace innovation and keynoted several conferences for the Institute of Management Consultants, the Project Management Institute, and *Inc.* Magazine. She appeared as an expert on workplace trends on the *NBC Nightly News, The Bloomberg Report*, Tech TV, KRON TV, NPR's TechNation, and KCBS radio. She was invited to serve as a panelist at the Aspen Institute forum on "The Future of Work." Earlier this year, she was a contributor to the Solo Project research report, *The Solo City*. In 2001, Marion published *A New Brand of Expertise: How Independent Consultants, Free Agents and Interim Managers Are Transforming the World of Work*.

Since 2013, Marion has been a director at the Alliance for CEOs. In that role, she facilitates peer-to-peer exchanges with CEO groups. Similarly, she has served as a mentor to three young CEOs in the human capital space and remains a regular advisor to these executives.

She was an adjunct professor at the University of San Francisco School of Management for seven years, teaching HR and management communications to both undergraduates and MBAs.

Marion is also an active board member. She is the audit chair of CPP Inc., a private publisher that owns the most widely used psychometric tool in the world, the Meyers Briggs Type Instrument. She is on the Board of the Front Porch, a California public benefit corporation that provides housing and services to residents of its senior living communities. She is a member of the National Association of Corporate Directors as well as the Society for Human Resource Management. She has also been member of YPO (the Young President's Organization) and its alumni organization, YPO Gold.

She has been a strong volunteer in the community as well. Marion currently serves as the chairman of the board of ReSurge International, a humanitarian NGO that sends reconstructive surgeons to help the poor and builds medical capacity in the developing world through its global training program. She has also served on the boards of the American Liver Foundation and the Hamilton Family Center, a homeless shelter for families in San Francisco.

Marion regularly posts on her blog, marionmcgovern.com. She lives in San Francisco, California, with her husband, Jerry, an attorney. They have three wonderful adult children and a mischievous Labrador puppy.